YEADON'S REGISTER

of

L N E R

LOCOMOTIVES

Volume Thirty-Five

Class J14, & J15

YEADON'S REGISTER OF L.N.E.R. LOCOMOTIVES - VOLUME 35.

EDITOR'S NOTE & ACKNOWLEDGEMENTS

It is some time since we published a Register which featured just two locomotive classes and this volume puts the spotlight on the former Great Eastern 0-6-0 tender engines which became LNER classes J14 and J15. The former, which actually came after the latter, was not as sucessful as its predecessor and did not last too long in the LNER scheme, indeed the GER themselves acknowledged the fact that the Holden designed 0-6-0 was nowhere near as good as the Worsdell 0-6-0 and started to scrap them long before Grouping.

It would have been ideal to have put the other former GER 0-6-0 tender engines within this volume too but space, or rather size, had to be considered. Including the classes J16 to J20 would have involved another ninety-six pages at least to give them all justice and the cost would have been prohibitive. So, those 'modern' GE 0-6-0's will have their own volume at a date not too far in the future.

Considering that Eric Fry has been retired from a 'normal job' for many years and that he has now put away his Editor's pen with the RCTS *Locomotives of the LNER* series, he does not stint on the enthusiasm put into making sure that each volume of the Register is as it should be - factual, accurate and historically correct. Where any doubt hovers, after exhaustive detective work, it is left out on the grounds that it is simply 'doubtful'.

Both Mike and Roy are to be thanked for the seemingly endless toil of bashing out the numbers and words which, when put together, make up the pages of the Register. Luckily word processing has made life easier for the 'setters' but accuracy is still foremost and paramount and WBY would have been very pleased with their efforts, just as we are.

The Archivist and staff at the University of Hull Archive are to be thanked for making us welcome and letting us get on with the task which they know will one day be complete.

Over in Ontario both Jean and Simon look forward to the completion of each volume as much as we do and they still apparently find amazement in the reproduction carried out by our printers The Amadeus Press up in Cleckheaton. They too must be thanked for the professionalism shown during the whole production process.

Once again the support of you the reader has enabled us to complete another volume in this epic series which started some seventy years ago when a certain Yorkshireman wanted to find out more about LNER locomotives.

The next *Yeadon's Register of LNER Locomotives*, Volume 36, contains the repair history of classes F1, F2, G1, G2, G3, G4, G7, G8, G9, and G10.

Material contained within this volume has the following catalogue references:
DYE/1/38; DYE/1/99.

The Yeadon Collection is available for inspection and anyone who wishes to inspect it should contact:-
The Archivist
Brynmor Jones Library
University of Hull
Hull
HU6 7RX
Tel: 01482-465265
A catalogue of the Yeadon collection is available.

First published in the United Kingdom by
BOOK LAW PUBLICATIONS 2005 in association with CHALLENGER
382 Carlton Hill, Nottingham, NG4 1JA.
Printed and bound by The Amadeus Press, Cleckheaton, West Yorkshire.

INTRODUCTION

The Great Eastern Railway tended to build small, lightweight locomotives to work the somewhat lightly built lines which made up a large proportion of its system. Right up to, and indeed well after Grouping some of the main and many of the secondary lines still had weight restrictions which would have a bearing on the longevity of one of the classes featured in this Register. Another factor to consider, and probably the most important because it concerns both of the classes under the microscope here, is a boiler which for nearly eighty years was one of the most reliable, compact and efficient produced by the GER.

J14

With a proven boiler at his disposal, the Great Eastern Locomotive Engineer of 1893, James Holden, set about to better the Y14 Worsdell design and at the same time bring further standardisation into GER locomotive policy by creating another similar 0-6-0 goods engine. Basically, Holden attempted to update the Y14 class (LNER J15) in the shape of the N31 class 0-6-0 (LNER J14), with a fresh arrangement of cylinders and valves although retaining the same boiler. Outwardly the two classes were similar except that the boilers on Class N31 were pitched 7½ inches higher than on Class Y14, the chimney being shortened accordingly.

Classified N31 on the GE, a single engine emerged from Stratford shops in the first month of 1893. It was quickly followed by ten more that year and from 1894 to 1898 another seventy N31's were built at Stratford. Unfortunately it took that long for the fact to sink in that the redesign had been a failure and that the original Y14 engines were markedly superior. Consequently the following year saw him building more Y14's to Worsdell's design (*see* below).

From the start the whole class carried the sloping grate version (LNER Diagram 32) of Worsdell's original design of boiler. In 1896 the original boiler pressure of 140 psi was raised to 160 psi on new boilers. All except the last ten engines were built with a butt jointed two-ring barrelled boiler. Later in 1898, Nos.562 to 571 (GER Order No.K43) and the last N31's built, got boilers which had two-ring telescopic barrels (*see also* J15). Replacement boilers also had this feature and by Grouping the eighteen survivors all had the telescopic barrel boilers.

Withdrawal of Class N31 began as early as 1908. During their comparatively short lifetime the only change of note was the substitution of the smokebox door for a heavier pattern from 1915 onwards on the survivors. Some of the engines carried braking euipment for working passenger stock.

Although Stratford was not 100% responsible for the maintenance of former GER locomotives during the first few years of the LNER, it is virtually certain that Stratford took care of the scrapping of the J14 class.

Only eighteen J14's survived to 1923, scattered about the former GER but mainly confined to yard work. Withdrawals took care of six in 1923, five went in 1924 and the last seven in 1925. By April the last two, Nos.981 and 987 had been condemned making class J14 extinct. All went to the scrapyard still carrying GER numbers. However, in September 1923 No.998 had been put on the Duplicate List, becoming 0998, to clear its number for a new Class N7 0-6-2T.

J15

Over the ten year period from 1883 to 1892 the Great Eastern Railway invested in no less than 229 Class Y14 0-6-0 goods tender engines to cope with its increasing goods and mineral traffic. All the class, except for nineteen engines supplied by Sharp, Stewart & Co. in 1884 and numbered 37 to 41, 119 to 124 and 592 to 599, were constructed at Stratford works to the design of T.W.Worsdell. In 1885 James Holden succeeded Worsdell but carried on building the Y14's probably because he recognised a good thing when he saw it. Nevertheless, in 1893 he was tempted into the belief that he could improve the design by substituting cylinders with valves below instead of between them, thus producing the N31 class mentioned above. This proved to be a disaster, but eighty-one engines of the modified design were turned out before the situation was acknowledged. In 1899 building of the class resumed under Holden, with thirty coming out during that year from Stratford. These were followed in 1906 by ten more. Six years later when S.D.Holden was in charge at Stratford and just prior to A.J.Hill taking the reins, another ten appeared followed in 1913 by a final batch of ten under the company's last Locomotive Engineer, bringing the total to 289.

The largest class on the GER and the largest class taken over by the LNER at Grouping, the J15's were designed in 1883 by the GE's fifth Locomotive Engineer with building perpetuated through the tenure's of the Company's next and final three Locomotive Engineer's. When the last engines of the class were withdrawn in 1962, the design was just a year short of eighty years old. All in all, the class was something of a tribute to its designer T.W.Worsdell.

The boiler used on the Y14's was adopted as standard by James Holden and used on his T19 class 2-4-0 (110 engines) from 1886,

Out of eighty-one engines built at Stratford from January 1893 to November 1898, only eighteen survived to become LNER J14 class at Grouping. No.992 had been taken out of stock in July 1921 but retained the original style plain dished smokebox door, flush with the front plate which was superseded from 1915 by a heavier pattern, as shown on page 4, bottom.

D27 class 2-2-2 (21 engines) from 1889, T26 class 2-4-0's (100 engines and LNER Class E4) from 1891, and C32 class 2-4-2T (50 engines and LNER Class F3) from 1893. Of course, another Holden design using the Y14 class boiler was the N31 class 0-6-0 tender engine of which eighty-one were turned out (*see* above). In all some 651 GER locomotives carried the same size boiler.

To give the reader some idea of this 'marvellous' little boiler, it was 4ft 4ins. in diameter and had a 10ft long, three-ring butt jointed barrel, with the dome situated on the middle ring. The firebox casing was some 6ft long with, initially, a level firegrate which had an area of 17.9 square feet. Working pressure was 140 psi.

Over the thirty year period of GER construction of these Worsdell designed boilers a few improvements appeared with probably the most significant change being the introduction, from 1891, of a sloping grate with an 18 sq. ft. area. No.895, new that year became the first J15 to have this type of boiler The boilers with sloping grates could not be fitted to the earlier engines and replacement boilers for them, with level grates, continued to be made. It was not until 1932 that the problem of maintaining two separate stocks of boilers for Class J15 was at last tackled and modification to the frames of the earlier engines began so that the newer pattern of boiler could be carried. The two types of boiler warranted separate Diagram numbers under the LNER and they were classified 31 and 32 respectively.

After thirty engines with the new type of boiler had been built during 1891, a more visible change was introduced on No.925 onwards which had a boiler barrel fabricated from two rings with the dome now sitting further forward on the front ring. The two ring barrel became standard for all of the smaller boilers constructed at Stratford, including, from 1893, the replacement boilers built for the earlier Y14's with flat grates. Like the N31's, the Y14 also had their boiler pressure raised in 1896 to 160 psi for both new and replacement boilers. In 1898 the last variant on the original boiler design was adopted; this involved the introduction of a telescopic two-ring barrel (still with the dome forward) and all new boiler construction from thereon came out in this fashion. The first Y14 to receive one of these boilers was No.507 of GER Order No.I45 in 1899. By Grouping all the J15's were running with boilers constructed from two rings and with 160 psi pressure. In addition to the above design changes there were various alterations to the number and size of the boiler tubes and this process continued under the LNER as late as 1940.

Until March 1914 Stratford numbered its boilers the same as the running number of the engine to which it was first fitted and up to that date interchanging of boilers did not take place. However, in the drive to reduce the time when locomotives were out of traffic in works, interchanging was introduced and became the normal procedure; spare boilers were therefore constructed to permit the scheme to work efficiently. At the same time a new range of boiler numbers was generated for all new boilers, with the old boilers keeping their original numbers. For classes J14 and J15 they were:

Diagram 31 (flat bottom firebox):	2300-2397 (J15 only).
Diagram 32 (sloping grate firebox*):	2500-2580 (J14, J15**).
	2650-2799 (J14, J15**).
	3300-3388 (J14, J15**).
	3394-3398 (J14, J15**).

* Known at Stratford as bevel bottom firebox boilers.
** Also E4 and F3 classes in LNER days.

To enable the later Diagram 32 type of boiler to be carried, the J15 engine frames needed a slight alteration which involved cutting back the base of the frames adjacent to the firebox area and adding a doubling piece to the remaining part to preserve strength. However, not all J15's had this modification and as can be gleaned from the tables, only Diagram 31 boilers were fitted to many. No

other class of locomotive carried the Diagram 31 boiler but replacement boilers of this type continued to be constructed until 1928. From 1932 it was decided to carry out the above modification if no Diagram 31 boiler was available when one of the pre-1890 J15's was in shops so that a Diagram 32 could be installed in its place. Eleven engines were altered almost immediately in 1932 and in all thirty-nine were so changed, the last in 1947 (No.5365, ex 7846). Although No.7843 was altered to carry a Diagram 32 in 1932, in 1944 it reverted to a Diagram 31 type which it kept to withdrawal. No modification was necessary to engines built to Diagram 32 standard to enable them to be fitted with Diagram 31 boilers. Between 1934 and 1948 a total of thirteen post-1891 engines carried Diagram 31 boilers (*see* following table), one of them No.7901 was twice fitted, once in 1937 and, as 65398 in 1948.

1934 -	7899, 7915.
1935 -	7943.
1936 -	7510, 7918.
1937 -	7509, 7514, 7901, 7913.
1938 -	7898.
1939 -	7924.
1940 -	7910.
1941 -	7512.
1948 -	65398.

Note: None of the dual-fitted engines ever ran with a Diagram 31 boiler.

The Diagram 31 boiler survived until June 1952 when No.65366 was withdrawn. Finally, like the J14's, none of the J15's were ever superheated or rebuilt with a bigger boiler.

Up to 1892 the Stratford built J15's were put into traffic with just a handbrake on the tender whereas those supplied by Sharp, Stewart in 1884 had steam brakes. Later, between 1896 and 1901, the Stratford built engines were fitted with steam brakes. In 1899, when construction of the class recommenced at Stratford, thirty engines were turned out between May and October and of these, twenty were fitted with steam brakes. The other ten, Nos.640 to 649 came out with Westinghouse equipment and the first five of this batch were also fitted with vacuum ejectors. The remaining five got this latter braking gear fitted by the LNER during 1931-32. The final thirty engines, built at the rate of ten a year in 1906, 1912 and 1913, all came into traffic with both Westinghouse and vacuum ejector gear. Only seven other members of the class got vacuum ejectors, all in the 1930's, and no more had Westinghouse fitted.

With a class constructed over a period of thirty years and having such a long life it is natural that many detail changes were introduced. In addition to those affecting the boiler and braking system, there were variations in the wheel type and siderods, boiler handrails, shape of cab side and cut outs, safety valves, smokebox doors, and pattern of tender attached, to name the most obvious. These features are described in the captions to the illustrations.

However, it was during LNER days that the most noticeable change occured. Until 1930 all the smaller GER engines carried stovepipe chimneys. In that year, when Edward Thompson was Mechanical Engineer at Stratford, he introduced the NER style of cast iron chimney as replacement for the old-fashioned looking stovepipe (not used elsewhere on the LNER) and surviving engines, including the J15's, were changed as they were shopped. A further change three years later involved replacing the low-pitched wooden cab roofs by new, more arched roofs made from steel plate.

During 1934-35 Nos.7512, 7523, 7888, 7911 and 7941 were given new cabs with a single side window, together with back cabs on the tender, in order to improve protection for the engine crews when working on the Colne Valley line where there were no turntables.

As mentioned in previous volumes concerning former Great Eastern locomotives (7, 14 and 30), the 1924 renumbering dates

Two hundred and eighty-nine engines were built as Class J15 from July 1883 to September 1913 of which two hundred and seventy-two were taken over by the LNER. Of the others, one had been withdrawn in August 1920 and the other sixteen between March and October 1922. The first thirty, Nos.610 to 639, were built at Stratford and apart from changes of detail were substantially as built when they became LNER engines. No.627 was as shown when ex works on 11th August 1923. Nos.619, 624, 626, 632 and 637 were amongst those withdrawn in 1922. Stratford.

are, in some cases, difficult to pin down especially for locomotives withdrawn prior to WW2. The absence of certain Stratford works registers and the disappearance of Engine History Cards (these latter items to apparently help the war effort) do nothing to enlighten us further with specific dates. Therefore, the tables may appear not to have the completeness given to other pre-Grouping classes.

Except for a few engines transferred to Doncaster, Mexborough and Barnsley during the 1939-45 war, the class was confined to sheds in East Anglia (including Lincoln which, of course, was GER territory) where they were to be seen on almost every branch line as well as on the main routes.

The apparent small size of the J15's, which was accentuated by the low pitch of the boiler, belied their undoubted ability to perform. In the LNER Freight Train Loads book they were shown as being in Group 3 (the groups ran from 1 to 8, the highest). This group included classes J6 and J11. Other 0-6-0's which ran in East Anglia were J3, J4 and J21 (Group 2) and J10 (Group 1). All these classes had a nominally greater tractive effort. In practice, the load book (in 1944) permitted Class J15 to take 50 empty wagons from Temple Mills to Cambridge, and 75 empties onwards to March. On the Up line, 33 loaded coal wagons or 49 goods could be taken to London. Even in early BR days it is known that a J15 took the place of a WD 2-8-0 on a through freight turn from King's Lynn to Temple Mills, load unrecorded. In 1953 No.65478 was noted hauling eleven LMS corridor coaches from Yarmouth Beach to Lowestoft.

Besides the works at Stratford maintaining the class, during 1923 the LNER also entrusted a number of J15 heavy repairs to engine sheds on the former GER system, Cambridge, Ipswich, Norwich and Peterborough East being the sheds involved. Darlington works also took care of four of the class giving them general repairs.

The first withdrawal took place in August 1920 when No.513 was condemned as a result of accident damage sustained whilst on active service for the Government. On the eve of Grouping another sixteen were condemned which meant that *only* two hundred and seventy-two J15's became LNER property. During the 1920's another forty-seven of the class were withdrawn and during the 1930's some ninety-five were scrapped. Wartime motive power requirements brought a stop to the withdrawals of the J15's and scrapping resumed once again after the end of the conflict.

Of the one hundred and twenty-seven which survived the LNER to become BR property, only seventy-one of the J15's lasted long enough to have 60000 added to their LNER numbers. Although the 1950's started out with some heavy withdrawals, during 1950 (12) and 1951 (15), the rest of that decade, up to 1958, was fairly considerate to the J15's with only a baker's dozen being condemned between 1952 and 1957 with none at all during 1953 and 1954. However, even the J15's could not last forever and in 1958 eleven of them were withdrawn, with fifteen more in 1959. The years of 1960 and 1961 saw fifteen more scrapped, leaving just eleven to see in the new year of 1962. By September the number of J15 class engines was down to four and on the 16th of that month all the other surviving former Great Eastern Railway locomotives still operational were condemned as British Railways slowly got rid of steam from the regions. One of the four J15's withdrawn that day was No.65361, a Stratford veteran dating from July 1889, whilst the other three were all 1912 built and it was from this trio that one engine was purchased for preservation by the Midland & Great Northern Joint Railway Preservation Society. No.65462 can be seen today on the North Norfolk Railway.

A remarkable coincidence was that 289 J15's were built, exactly the same total as Gresley's J39 class.

Nos.970, 973, 976, 977 and 978, built in 1894, had tenders taken from the Bromley 7ft 6in. 4-2-2 engines which had been withdrawn. These tenders could be recognised by their hemispherical frame slots and separate rear footsteps. Note the plain grey livery with 19in. yellow painted numbers.

The more usual tender for this class was the Holden 2640 gallons type which had frame slots with parallel top and bottom edges and semi-circular ends. None of the J14 tenders acquired coal guards on their top edges.

CLASS J 14

(7)980

Stratford.

To traffic 10/1893.

REPAIRS:
Str. 2/3—16/8/05.**G.**
Str. 31/8/20—14/1/21.**G.**

BOILERS:
980.
980 16/8/05.
970 14/1/21.

SHED:
Ilford.

CONDEMNED: 20/9/23.

(7)981

Stratford.

To traffic 10/1893.

REPAIRS:
Str. ?/?—?/6/05.**G.**
Str. 7/3/19—23/1/20.**G.**

BOILERS:
981.
981 ?/6/05.

SHED:
Stratford.

CONDEMNED: 1/4/25.

(7)983

Stratford.

To traffic 10/1893.

REPAIRS:
Str. ?/?—?/12/05.**G.**
Str. 25/10/18—24/7/19.**G.**
Str. 20/8/21—5/1/22.**G.**

BOILERS:
983.
983 ?/12/05.
2665 24/7/19.

SHED:
Parkeston.

CONDEMNED: 13/1/25.

(7)984

Stratford.

To traffic 10/1893.

REPAIRS:
Str. 13/11/05—19/4/06.**G.**
Str. 12/5—15/12/22.**G.**

BOILERS:
984.
984 19/4/06.
978 15/12/22.

SHED:
Ipswich.

CONDEMNED: 25/2/25.

(7)985

Stratford.

To traffic 10/1893.

REPAIRS:
Str. 30/11/04—18/5/05.**G.**
Str. 27/4—12/10/17.**G.**

BOILERS:
985.
985 18/5/05.
2672 12/10/17.

SHED:
Stratford.

CONDEMNED: 14/12/23.

(7)987

Stratford.

To traffic 10/1893.

REPAIRS:
Str. 23/3—17/8/06.**G.**
Str. 6/9—23/12/22.**G.**

BOILERS:
987.
987 17/8/06.
441 23/12/22.

SHED:
Stratford.

CONDEMNED: 1/4/25.

(7)993

Stratford.

To traffic 7/1894.

REPAIRS:
Str. 8/2—19/7/07.**G.**
Str. 14/12/17—7/6/18.**G.**

BOILERS:
993.
993 19/7/07.
2680 7/6/18.

SHED:
March.

CONDEMNED: 18/8/23.

(7)998

Stratford.

To traffic 7/1894.

REPAIRS:
Str. ?/?—?/6/06.**G.**
Str. 29/11/18—2/1/20.**G.**

BOILERS:
998.
998 ?/6/06.
503 2/1/20.

SHED:
Norwich.

RENUMBERED:
0998 ?/9/23.

CONDEMNED: 27/3/25.

(7)970

Stratford.

To traffic 8/1894.

REPAIRS:
Str. 13/7—31/12/08.**G.**
Str. 7/8—30/9/20.**G.**

BOILERS:
970.
970 31/12/08.
604 30/9/20.

SHED:
King's Lynn.

CONDEMNED: 21/12/23.

(7)973

Stratford.

To traffic 8/1894.

REPAIRS:
Str. 29/4—11/11/08.**G.**
Str. 18/3—14/9/21.**G.**

BOILERS:
973.
973 11/11/08.

SHED:
King's Lynn.

CONDEMNED: 4/3/25.

(7)976

Stratford.

To traffic 8/1894.

REPAIRS:
Str. 7/7/08—3/2/09.**G.**
Str. 10/12/20—29/4/21.**G.**

BOILERS:
976.
976 3/2/09.

SHED:
Colchester.

CONDEMNED: 18/8/23.

(7)977

Stratford.

To traffic 10/1894.

REPAIRS:
Str. 9/1—28/6/07.**G.**
Str. 6/1—3/6/15.**G.**
Str. 12/7/18—20/5/19.**G.**

BOILERS:
977.
977 28/6/07.

(7)977 cont./
946 3/6/15.

SHED:
Colchester.

CONDEMNED: 3/1/24.

---

(7)978

Stratford.

To traffic 10/1894.
REPAIRS:
Str. ?/?—?/12/08.**G.**
Str. 6/1—31/3/22.**G.**

BOILERS:
978.
978 ?/12/08.
992 31/3/22.

SHED:
Colchester.

CONDEMNED: 17/7/24.

---

(7)959

Stratford.

To traffic 11/1896.

REPAIRS:
Str. 17/7—17/11/05.**G.**
Str. 7/1—26/7/21.**G.**

BOILERS:
959.
959 17/11/05.

SHED:
Colchester.

CONDEMNED: 21/12/23.

---

(7)963

Stratford.

To traffic 12/1896.

REPAIRS:
Str. ?/?—?/6/07.**G.**
Str. 28/12/17—5/4/18.**G.**
*Hole through boiler. Hit by a
British A.A. shell during an air
raid 18th December 1917.*

BOILERS:
963.
963 ?/6/07.

SHED:
Peterborough East.

CONDEMNED: 14/7/24.

---

(7)964

Stratford.

To traffic 12/1896.

REPAIRS:
Str. 9/11/07—5/3/08.**G.**
Str. 22/11/18—24/10/19.**G.**

BOILERS:
964.
964 5/3/08.

SHED:
Yarmouth.

CONDEMNED: 16/2/24.

---

(7)951

Stratford.

To traffic 7/1897.

REPAIRS:
Str. ?/?—?/6/08.**G.**
Str. 21/1—14/10/21.**G.**

BOILERS:
951.
951 ?/6/08.
2721 14/10/21.

SHED:
Sudbury.

CONDEMNED 6/2/24.

---

(7)604

Stratford.

To traffic 10/1897.

REPAIRS:
Str. 21/12/06—31/5/07.**G.**
Str. 25/3—7/7/20.**G.**

BOILERS:
604.
604 31/5/07.
998 7/7/20.

SHED:
Stratford.

CONDEMNED: 27/3/25.

**The heavier type of smokebox with a flat flange was fitted from 1915 when replacements were needed and most of the LNER engines
had acquired them. Stratford works, 25th March 1925.**

Nos.971, 981, 986 and the last forty built, had only a steam brake on the engine with no provision for train braking. Nos.981 and 987, withdrawn on 1st April 1925, were the last of the class, none of which had any repair or painting after Grouping. No.981 acquired this Worsdell 3066 gallon tender in 1912. Stratford shed, 28th February 1925

For working excursion trains, Nos.964, 965, 966, 967, 968, and 989 to 998 were fitted, when built, with the Westinghouse brake both on the engine and for train braking. In September 1923 No.998 was put on the Duplicate List, its number being required for a new N7 class engine. It retained its brass number plates with a cypher painted above them and also had a 19in. size 0998 painted on the tender. Norwich, 8th March 1925.

Five more, numbered 959 to 963, had Westinghouse brake plus vacuum ejector for train braking, but only Nos.959 and 963 survived to become LNER locomotives. Stratford shed.

All had, and retained, a stovepipe chimney. The safety valves were of the Ramsbottom type in an enclosure with which the whistle mounting was also combined. Stratford works, 24th May 1923.

Nos.959 to 968 built in 1896, were first fitted with a 2500 gallons tenders with frames cut away in an arc between the axles and with sides made of three panels. These tenders had been reconstructed after being used with Adams "Ironclad" 4-4-0 engines. Colchester shed, March 1913.

The next batch of nineteen, Nos.37 to 41, 119 to 124 and 592 to 599, were built by Sharp, Stewart & Co., Manchester between April and July 1884 to the same design. On 30th June 1912, No.41 was renumbered 600. Nos.40 and 123 of the batch did not become LNER property. Stratford shed, 18th July 1923.

All the other two hundred and forty were built at Stratford from February 1885 to September 1913, and only Nos.687, 695, 804, 808, 811, 822, 882, 884, 885 in 1922 and 513 in August 1920 had been withdrawn before Grouping. No.887 is as ex works 17th May 1922.

Engines built before 1891 had a level grate in the firebox and these boilers were given Diagram No.31 by the LNER. They could only be used on the J15 class but, continued to be built until the end of 1928 and the last one in service came off No.65366 (ex7847) when that engine and its boiler were withdrawn on 2nd June 1952. Stratford, 13th March 1927.

CLASS J 15

7610

Stratford.

To traffic 7/1883.

REPAIRS:
Str. 22/12/07—17/3/08.**G.**
Str. 6/4—26/6/25.**G.**
Str. ?/?—?/10/27.**G.**
Coal guard on tender.

BOILERS:
610.
630 26/6/25.

SHEDS:
Norwich.
March 20/10/26.

RENUMBERED:
7610 26/6/25.

CONDEMNED: 2/10/29.

7611

Stratford.

To traffic 7/1883.

REPAIRS:
Str. ?/?—?/6/10.**G.**
Str. 22/11/17—22/3/18.**G.**

BOILERS:
611.
611 ?/6/10.
2335 22/3/18.

SHED:
Norwich.

RENUMBERED:
7611 ?/?

CONDEMNED: 14/8/26.

7612

Stratford.

To traffic 7/1883.

REPAIRS:
Str. 7/10/07—5/2/08.**G.**
Nor. ?/?—?/12/23.**H.**
Str. 12/11/24—31/1/25.**G.**
Str. 14/12/29—7/1/30.**G.**
Coal guard on tender.

BOILERS:
612.
612 5/2/08.
810 31/1/25.
2329 7/1/30.

SHEDS:
Norwich.
March 19/10/26.

RENUMBERED:
7612 31/1/25.

CONDEMNED: 25/1/32.

7613

Stratford.

To traffic 7/1883.

REPAIRS:
???. 24/3—16/9/98.**G.**
Str. ?/?—?/2/12.**G.**
Str. 5/9/19—6/1/20.**G.**
Str. ?/?—?/11/28.**G.**
Coal guard on tender.

BOILERS:
613.
613 ?/2/12.
2350 6/1/20.
2361 ?/11/28.

SHEDS:
Lowestoft.
Yarmouth ?/?/?.
Norwich 30/9/28.

RENUMBERED:
7613 ?/?

CONDEMNED: 3/6/31.

7614

Stratford.

To traffic 8/1883.

REPAIRS:
Str. ?/?—?/6/06.**G.**
Str. 5/9/19—2/1/20.**G.**

BOILERS:
614.
614 ?/6/06.
2353 2/1/20.

SHED:
Norwich (Wells-next-the-sea).

RENUMBERED:
7614 ?/?

CONDEMNED: 11/9/26.

7615

Stratford.

To traffic 9/1883.

REPAIRS:
Str. ?/?—?/12/08.**G.**
Nor. ?/?—?/7/21.**H.**
Str. 30/8—31/12/23.**G.**

BOILERS:
615.
615 ?/12/08.
851 31/12/23.

SHED:
Norwich.

RENUMBERED:
7615 ?/?

CONDEMNED: 18/10/26.

7616

Stratford.

To traffic 9/1883.

REPAIRS:
Str. 25/2—28/8/07.**G.**
Str. 30/4—12/12/19.**G.**
Str. 6/5—27/7/27.**G.**

BOILERS:
616.
616 28/8/07.
2351 12/12/19.
2352 27/7/27.

SHEDS:
Norwich.
March 20/10/26.

RENUMBERED:
7616 ?/?

CONDEMNED: 13/7/29.

7617

Stratford.

To traffic 9/1883.

REPAIRS:
Str. ?/?—?/12/06.**G.**
Str. 10/10/23—4/1/24.**G.**

BOILERS:
617.
617 ?/12/06.
805 4/1/24.

SHED:
Norwich.

RENUMBERED:
7617 ??

CONDEMNED: 27/10/26.

7618

Stratford.

To traffic 10/1883.

REPAIRS:
Str. 3/2—25/4/11.**G.**
Str. 23/1—9/4/20.**G.**
Str. 19/12/23—9/4/24.**G.**

BOILERS:
618.
618 25/4/11.

WORKS CODES:- Cam - Cambridge shed. Dar - Darlington. Don - Doncaster. Ips - Ipwich shed. Nor - Norwich shed. Pbo - Peterborough East shed. Str - Stratford.
REPAIR CODES:- **C/H** - Casual Heavy. **C/L** - Casual Light. **G** - General. **H**- Heavy. **H/I** - Heavy Intermediate. **L** - Light. **L/I** - Light Intermediate. **N/C** - Non-Classified.

7618 cont./
  625 9/4/20.
  2306 9/4/24.

SHEDS:
Lincoln.
Norwich ?/?/?.
Ipswich 11/3/27.

RENUMBERED:
7618 9/4/24.

CONDEMNED: 17/7/29.

_____

7620

Stratford.

To traffic 3/1884.

REPAIRS:
Str. ?/?—?/6/08.**G.**
Str. 18/5—23/9/21.**G.**
Str. 23/2—8/5/24.**G.**

BOILERS:
  620.
  620 ?/6/08.
  698 23/9/21.
  2320 8/5/24.

SHED:
Norwich.

RENUMBERED:
7620 8/5/24.

CONDEMNED: 29/10/26.

_____

7621

Stratford.

To traffic 3/1884.

REPAIRS:
Str. 2/10/06—30/1/07.**G.**
Str. 25/11/15—15/4/16.**G.**
Str. 6/4—29/9/23.**G.**
Str. 25/11/27—22/2/28.**G.**
Coal guard on tender.
Str. 18/3—3/4/30.**G.**

BOILERS:
  621.
  621 30/1/07.
  2323 15/4/16.
  2322 29/9/23.
  2377 22/2/28.
  2389 3/4/30.

SHEDS:
Peterborough East.

Yarmouth 14/11/28.
Peterborough East 21/1/29.
March 1/9/29.

RENUMBERED:
7621 ?/?

CONDEMNED: 4/7/32.

_____

7622

Stratford.

To traffic 3/1884.

REPAIRS:
Str. 31/3—23/8/06.**G.**
Str. 8/2—16/7/18.**G.**
Str. 7/9—5/12/23.**G.**

BOILERS:
  622.
  622 23/8/06.
  855 16/7/18.
  2346 5/12/23.

SHED:
Stratford.

RENUMBERED:
7622 ?/?

CONDEMNED: 12/10/26.

_____

7623

Stratford.

To traffic 3/1884.

REPAIRS:
Str. 10/12/06—23/4/07.**G.**
Str. 24/2—27/5/21.**G.**
Str. 30/4—25/9/26.**G.**
Coal guard on tender.
Str. 28/8—19/10/28.**G.**
Str. 9—24/10/30.**G.**

BOILERS:
  623.
  623 23/4/07.
  2314 27/5/21.
  2342 25/9/26.
  2363 19/10/28.
  2323 24/10/30.

SHED:
Stratford.

RENUMBERED:
7623 ?/?

CONDEMNED: 24/7/33.

7625

Stratford.

To traffic 3/1884.

REPAIRS:
Str. ?/?—?/12/09.**G.**
Str. 11/11/19—12/2/20.**G.**
Str. 17/2—17/5/23.**G.**
Str. 30/1—23/4/25.**G.**
Str. 18/2—1/3/30.**G.**
Coal guard on tender.

BOILERS:
  625.
  625 ?/12/09.
  2344 12/2/20.
  691 17/5/23.
  2330 23/4/25.
  2334 1/3/30.

SHEDS:
King's Lynn.
Cambridge 20/10/28.

RENUMBERED:
7625 23/4/25.

CONDEMNED: 1/6/32.

_____

7627

Stratford.

To traffic 3/1884.

REPAIRS:
Str. 6/4—11/8/11.**G.**
Str. 19/1—11/8/23.**G.**
Str. ?/?—?/3/25.**G.**
Str. ?/?—?/10/27.**G.**
Coal guard on tender.
Str. 10/2—15/3/30.**G.**

BOILERS:
  627.
  627 11/8/11.
  841 ?/3/25.
  2337 15/3/30.

SHEDS:
March.
King's Lynn ?/?/?.

RENUMBERED:
7627 ?/3/25.

CONDEMNED: 3/11/33.

_____

7628

Stratford.

To traffic 3/1884.

REPAIRS:
Str. 17/3—9/9/09.**G.**
Str. 2/7—20/12/18.**G.**
Str. 9/6—11/11/22.**G.**
???. 22/12/22—13/1/23.**H.**
Str. ?/?—?/3/25.**G.**
Str. ?/?—?/9/27.**G.**
Str. 24/2—15/3/30.**G.**
Coal guard on tender.

BOILERS:
  628.
  628 9/9/09.
  2347 20/12/18.
  2334 11/11/22.
  39 ?/3/25.
  2310 15/3/30.

SHEDS:
March.
Norwich ?/?/?.
Ipswich 1/12/28.

RENUMBERED:
7628 ?/3/25.

CONDEMNED: 21/12/31.

_____

7629

Stratford.

To traffic 3/1884.

REPAIRS:
Str. 28/12/12—6/6/13.**G.**
Str. 22/12/20—15/4/21.**G.**
Nor. ?/?—?/9/23.**H.**

BOILERS:
629.
629 6/6/13.
697 15/4/21.

SHED:
Norwich.

RENUMBERED:
7629 ?/?

CONDEMNED: 4/9/26.

_____

Beginning with No.895, built September 1891, the firebox now had a sloping grate and such boilers became LNER Diagram 32. They could also be used by classes E4 and F3, in which there were another one hundred and fifty engines. From 1932 alterations were made to thirty-nine pre 1891 engines to enable them to take Diagram 32 boilers. A small portion of the frame between the middle and rear wheels had to be removed to clear the washout plugs and a doubling piece with an aperture was then riveted on to give reinforcement. No.7833 was so altered when ex works 10th June 1937. Peterborough, 5th September 1937.

(right) After Grouping, four of the class went to Darlington works for general repair: Nos.683ᴇ (29th October 1923), 886ᴇ (29th October 1923), 635ᴇ (31st October 1923), and 892ᴇ (12th January 1924). In addition to the suffix which was applied, Darlington put Class Y14 on the front buffer beam, which was their GER classification but was never put on by Stratford works.

(below) The early Stratford built engines, Nos.7610 to 7639, had cast iron wheels without any balance weights, and only from 1899 were wheels balanced.

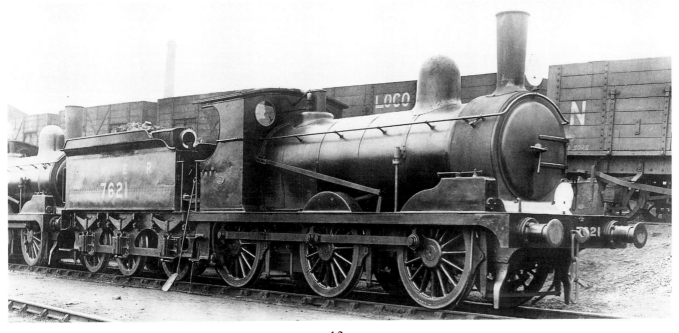

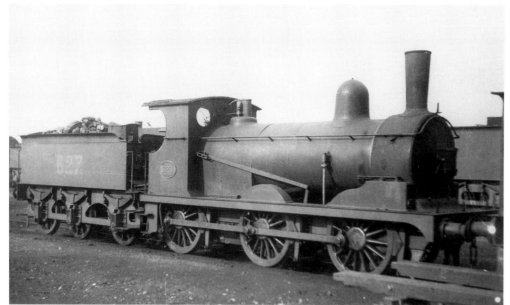

On the Sharp Stewart built engines, wrought iron wheels were used and these did not have balance weights either. Note LNER load class 3 plate fixed on the front buffer beam, the alternative position when there was no vacuum standpipe on which to put it. Stratford works, 18th March 1923.

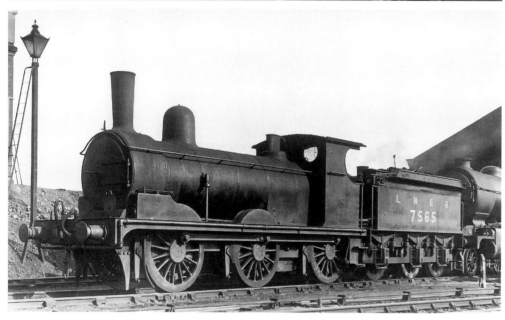

Only the final forty, Nos.640 to 649 and 542 to 571, had cast steel wheels with integral balance weights in them.

The last thirty engines, Nos.542 to 571 differed from the earlier engines by having fluted instead of flat coupling rods.

7630

Stratford.

To traffic 5/1884.

REPAIRS:
Str. 12/4—11/9/07.**G.**
Str. 4/2—29/4/16.**G.**
Str. 4/1—10/4/24.**G.**

BOILERS:
630.
630 11/9/07.
2324 29/4/16.
2315 10/4/24.

SHEDS:
Norwich.
Parkeston 1/12/28.

RENUMBERED:
7630 10/4/24.

CONDEMNED: 20/6/29.

_____

7631

Stratford.

To traffic 5/1884.

REPAIRS:
Str. ?/?—?/6/07.**G.**
Str. 1/12/22—14/3/23.**G.**
Str. 27/4—24/7/25.**G.**
Str. ?/?—?/6/28.**G.**
Coal guard on tender.
Str. 12/2—7/3/31.**G.**

BOILERS:
631.
631 ?/6/07.
804 14/3/23.
121 24/7/25.
846 7/3/31.

SHEDS:
Lowestoft.
Norwich ?/?/?.
Yarmouth 30/9/28.
Norwich 3/8/30.

RENUMBERED:
7631 24/7/25.

CONDEMNED: 13/12/33.

_____

7633

Stratford.

To traffic 6/1884.

REPAIRS:
Str. ?/?—?/12/03.**G.**
Str. 17/1—22/8/19.**G.**

BOILERS:
633.
633 ?/12/03.
628 22/8/19.

SHED:
Norwich.

RENUMBERED:
7633 ?/?

CONDEMNED: 14/8/26.

_____

7634

Stratford.

To traffic 6/1884.

REPAIRS:
Str. 16/12/07—3/3/08.**G.**
Str. 27/3—24/7/24.**G.**

BOILERS:
634.
634 3/3/08.

SHEDS:
Norwich.
Parkeston 6/3/28.

RENUMBERED:
7634 24/7/24.

CONDEMNED: 12/1/29.

_____

7635

Stratford.

To traffic 6/1884.

REPAIRS:
Str. 15/11/11—23/4/12.**G.**
Str. 20/6—28/9/21.**G.**
Dar. 2/7—31/10/23.**G.**
Str. 13/1—7/4/26.**G.**
Str. ?/?—?/9/28.**G.**
Coal guard on tender.
Str. 22/8—12/9/30.**G.**
Str. 29/9—14/10/32.**G.**

BOILERS:
635.
635 23/4/12.
2369 28/9/21.
2307 7/4/26.
2309 12/9/30.
2392 14/10/32.

SHEDS:
Yarmouth.
Ipswich ?/?/?.
Stratford 20/9/27.
Norwich 7/2/33.
Lowestoft 26/2/33.
Norwich 29/3/36.

RENUMBERED:
635ᴇ 31/10/23.
7635 7/4/26.

CONDEMNED: 30/4/36.

_____

7636

Stratford.

To traffic 6/1884.

REPAIRS:
Str. ?/?—?/11/03.**G.**
Str. 12/4—17/8/21.**G.**

BOILERS:
636.
636 ?/11/03.
2367 17/8/21.

SHEDS:
Yarmouth.
Norwich ?/?/?.
Colchester 1/12/28.

RENUMBERED:
7636 ?/?

CONDEMNED: 27/5/29.

_____

7638

Stratford.

To traffic 7/1884.

REPAIRS:
Str. ?/?—?/6/03.**G.**
Str. 30/1—13/4/20.**G.**
Str. 15/8—4/11/24.**G.**
Str. ?/?—?/4/26.**G.**
Str. ?/?—?/1/28.**G.**
Coal guard on tender.
Str. 20/5—6/6/30.**G.**
Str. 23/5—9/6/33.**G.**

BOILERS:
638.
638 ?/6/03.
599 13/4/20.
2381 ?/4/26.
2380 6/6/30.
2313 9/6/33.

SHED:
Norwich.

RENUMBERED:
7638 4/11/24.

CONDEMNED: 30/6/36.

_____

7639

Stratford.

To traffic 8/1884.

REPAIRS:
Str. 13/10/04—18/4/05.**G.**
Str. 27/4—29/9/23.**G.**

BOILERS:
639.
639 18/4/05.
2323 29/9/23.

SHEDS:
Norwich (Wells-next-the-sea).
Cambridge ?/?/?.
Norwich 12/12/25.
Stratford 13/3/26.

RENUMBERED:
7639 ?/?

CONDEMNED: 13/6/28.

_____

(070)37

Sharp Stewart 3146.

To traffic 4/1884.

REPAIRS:
Str. ?/?—?/4/07.**G.**
Str. ?/?—?/2/21.**G.**

BOILERS:
37.
37 ?/4/07.
124 ?/2/21.

SHED:
Ipswich.

CONDEMNED: 31/8/23.

_____

07038

Sharp Stewart 3147.

To traffic 4/1884.

REPAIRS:
Str. 29/11/05—2/3/06.**G.**

07038 cont./
Str. 11/3—10/5/21.**G.**
Str. 13/10—15/12/23.**G.**
Str. 19/2—25/6/26.**G.**
Str. 5/8—18/10/27.**G.**
Str. 7/4—2/5/30.**G.**

BOILERS:
  38.
   38 2/3/06.
2366 10/5/21.
  855 15/12/23.
  861 25/6/26.
  620 18/10/27.
2349 2/5/30.

SHED:
Bury St Edmunds.

RENUMBERED:
  038 ?/9/23.
07038 25/6/26 ???

CONDEMNED: 30/9/32.

_____

07039

Sharp Stewart 3148.

To traffic 4/1884.

REPAIRS:
Str. 7/3—19/8/08.**G.**
Str. 7/11/19—3/3/20.**G.**
Str. 29/9/22—26/1/23.**G.**
Str. ?/?—17/1/25.**G.**
Str. ?/?—?/3/28.**G.**
Coal guard on tender.
Str. 11/8—5/9/30.**G.**

BOILERS:
  39.
   39 19/8/08.
2316 3/3/20.
  535 26/1/23.
  119 17/1/25.
  691 5/9/30.

SHED:
Ipswich.

RENUMBERED:
  039 ?/9/23.
07039 17/1/25

CONDEMNED: 1/3/33.

_____

7600

Sharp Stewart 3150.

To traffic 4/1884.

REPAIRS:
Str. 15/12/10—21/3/11.**G.**
Str. 1/5—3/10/23.**G.**
Str. 12/7—27/9/28.**G.**
Coal guard on tender.
Str. 5—22/1/31.**G.**

BOILERS:
  41.
  600 21/3/11.
  803 3/10/23.
2368 27/9/28.
2340 22/1/31.

SHED:
Colchester.

RENUMBERED:
  600 *from* **41** *on* 30/6/12.
7600 ???

CONDEMNED: 18/6/34.

_____

7119

Sharp Stewart 3151.

To traffic 5/1884.

REPAIRS:
Str. 3/11/06—10/4/07.**G.**
Str. 29/9—31/12/21.**G.**
Str. 7/5—5/8/27.**G.**

BOILERS:
119.
119 10/4/07.
635 31/12/21.
598 5/8/27.

SHEDS:
Lowestoft.
Ipswich ?/?/?.

RENUMBERED:
7119 ????

CONDEMNED: 2/9/29.

_____

7120

Sharp Stewart 3152.

To traffic 5/1884.

REPAIRS:
Str. 3/11/06—19/4/07.**G.**
Str. 10/2—27/5/26.**G.**

BOILERS:
120.
120 19/4/07.
615 27/5/26.

SHED:
Norwich.

RENUMBERED:
7120 27/5/26 ???

CONDEMNED: 18/2/28.

_____

7121

Sharp Stewart 3153.

To traffic 5/1884.

REPAIRS:
Str. 22/12/08—11/5/09.**G.**
Str. 20/1—15/4/20.**G.**
Str. 21/6—16/10/24.**G.**
Str. 25/3—25/4/30.**G.**

BOILERS:
  121.
  121 11/5/09.
  810 15/4/20.
2302 16/10/24.
  877 25/4/30.

SHEDS:
Lowestoft.
Norwich 20/2/30.
Lowestoft 25/5/30.

RENUMBERED:
7121 16/10/24.

CONDEMNED: 1/3/33.

_____

7122

Sharp Stewart 3154.

To traffic 5/1884.

REPAIRS:
Str. 29/11/09—24/3/10.**G.**
Str. 20/10—31/12/20.**G.**
Str. ?/?—?/10/27.**G.**

BOILERS:
  122.
  122 24/3/10.
2359 31/12/20.
  890 ?/10/27.

SHED:
Lowestoft.

RENUMBERED:
7122 ????

CONDEMNED: 10/1/30.

_____

7124

Sharp Stewart 3156.

To traffic 5/1884.

REPAIRS:
Str. 15/5—22/8/13.**G.**
Str. 14/9—3/12/20.**G.**
Str. 14/7—27/9/27.**G.**
Str. 12/6—4/7/30.**G.**

BOILERS:
  124.
  124 22/8/13.
2356 3/12/20.
  839 27/9/27.
2308 4/7/30.

SHEDS:
Lowestoft.
Norwich 27/7/30.
Lowestoft *by* 3/32.

RENUMBERED:
7124 ???

CONDEMNED: 7/7/33.

_____

7592

Sharp Stewart 3157.

To traffic 5/1884.

REPAIRS:
Str. 21/9/04—29/3/05.**G.**
Str. 21/1—13/4/21.**G.**
Str. ?/?—?/11/23.**G.**
Str. 27/2—30/6/26.**G.**

BOILERS:
592.
592 29/3/05.
 37 13/4/21.
815 ?/11/23.
625 30/6/26.

SHED:
Ipswich.

RENUMBERED:
7592 ???

CONDEMNED: 31/8/28.

_____

Some interchanging of coupling rods did take place, and flat rods were used later on some of the Nos.7542 to 7571 batch.

In most cases, engines of the earlier batches, particularly those without train brakes, kept their flat rods.

There were of course a few cases of the earlier engines being fitted with fluted rods, mainly on those which had train brakes.

The smokebox door fitted at first was a plain dished type, fitting flush with the front plate and there was a separate handrail over the door.

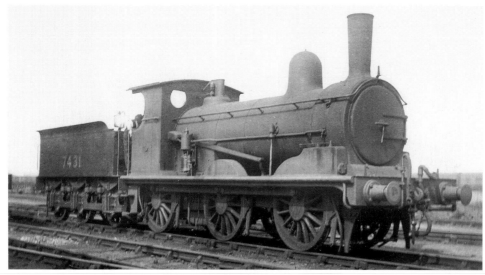

From 1915 a stronger, heavier door with a flat flange was introduced and all seem to have had it by the time they got their LNER numbers. At the same time, the separate handrails were replaced by a continuous type. This is J15 No.7643 with tender No.T7431. The reason for this coupling was because T7643 was damaged and engine No.7431 had been withdrawn. Stratford works, 14th July 1926.

At the right hand end of the front buffer beam some had twin lamp irons fitted to cater for the Great Northern Railway London area lamp codes as to the class of train. Although redundant by Grouping, 7522 and 7801 continued to carry the extra irons, as did No.65435 to its withdrawal on 15th October 1956 (*see* page 94, top), and No.65390 to 13th December 1958.

The two hundred and twenty-nine engines built to November 1892 had deep cut-outs in their cab side sheets.

The sixty built from 1899 had a shallower cut-out so as to match the side panel of the 2640 gallon capacity tender.

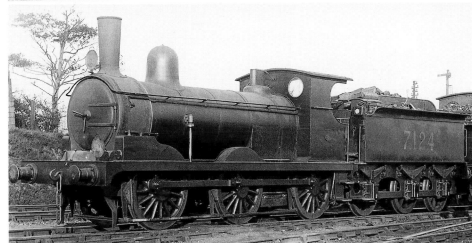

Until after Grouping, a Macallan variable blast pipe was fitted. This was controlled from the cab by the rod to the crank on the side of the smokebox.

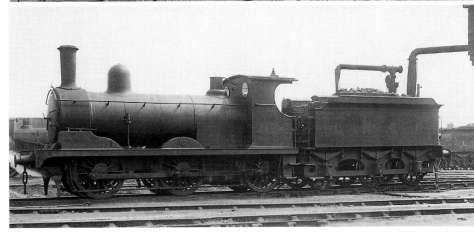

From 1925 the Macallan blastpipe was discarded and at the next shopping that apparatus was taken off.

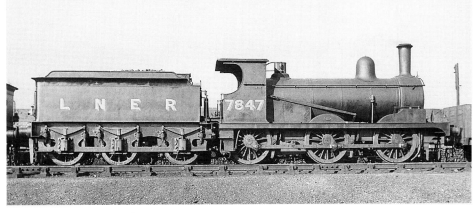

Various types of tube cleaners were tried on this class, although there was no external evidence of any of them. No.7847 carried a Parry soot blower from 5th May 1934 to 31st December 1936, so had it in this 16th June 1935 photograph. March shed.

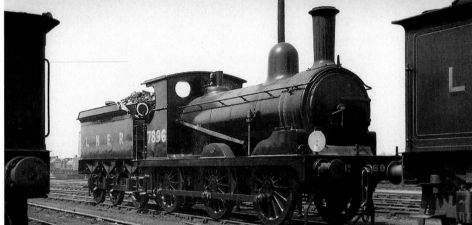

(above) When built, the whole class had the usual GER stovepipe chimney with a round beading at the rim, and No.7806, one of the last to carry that type, still had it until it went to works on 23rd December 1935. Stratford shed.

(left) Beginning in 1930, the stovepipe was replaced by a cast chimney of North Eastern Railway design, and by 1936 this change was completed. The height from rail was the same for both types - 12ft 11ins.

During the 1939-45 war the stovepipe re-appeared in the form of emergency repairs, riveted on to the existing base. These stovepipes did not taper as much as the originals.

Some of these wartime efforts were not very durable and by 1947 were having to be patched.

7593

Sharp Stewart 3158.

To traffic 6/1884.

REPAIRS:
Str. 18/9/06—9/1/07.**G.**
Str. 8/11/18—14/5/19.**G.**
Str. 14/3—22/5/22.**G.**
Str. 25/8—18/11/24.**G.**

BOILERS:
593.
593 9/1/07.
626 14/5/19.
2373 22/5/22.
802 18/11/24.

SHED:
Ipswich.

RENUMBERED:
7593 18/11/24.

CONDEMNED: 20/12/26.

7594

Sharp Stewart 3159.

To traffic 6/1884.

REPAIRS:
Str. 23/7/04—10/1/05.**G.**
Str. 7/3—11/7/19.**G.**
Str. 20/5—30/11/21.**G.**
Str. 4/4—23/6/24.**G.**

BOILERS:
594.
594 10/1/05.
598 11/7/19.
883 30/11/21.

SHED:
Ipswich.

RENUMBERED:
7594 23/6/24.

CONDEMNED: 24/7/26.

7595

Sharp Stewart 3160.

To traffic 6/1884.

REPAIRS:
Str. ?/?—?/12/07.**G.**
Str. 7/3—22/8/19.**G.**
Str. 25/1—18/3/22.**G.**

Str. 11/7—28/10/24.**G.**
Str. 4/2—14/4/27.**G.**

BOILERS:
595.
595 ?/12/07.
694 22/8/19.
2370 18/3/22.
2375 14/4/27.

SHED:
Ipswich.

RENUMBERED:
7595 28/10/24.

CONDEMNED: 28/6/29.

7596

Sharp Stewart 3161.

To traffic 7/1884.

REPAIRS:
Str. 3/3—24/8/05.**G.**
Str. 24/5—15/11/18.**G.**
Str. 18/1—2/6/23.**G.**
Str. ?/?—?/11/25.**G.**
Str. ?/?—?/5/28.**G.**
Coal guard on tender.
Str. 6—29/10/30.**G.**

BOILERS:
596.
596 24/8/05.
865 15/11/18.
2318 2/6/23.
2340 ?/11/25.
825 29/10/30.

SHED:
Bury St Edmunds.

RENUMBERED:
7596 ?/11/25 ???

CONDEMNED: 25/11/32.

7597

Sharp Stewart 3162.

To traffic 7/1884.

REPAIRS:
Str. ?/?—?/12/08.**G.**
Str. 10/12/20—16/4/21.**G.**
Str. 18/5—22/9/23.**G.**
Str. 9/7—16/11/25.**G.**

BOILERS:
597.

597 ?/12/08.
122 16/4/21.
614 22/9/23.
694 16/11/25.

SHED:
Ipswich.

RENUMBERED:
7597 16/11/25.

CONDEMNED: 27/4/28.

7598

Sharp Stewart 3163.

To traffic 7/1884.

REPAIRS:
Str. ?/?—?/12/07.**G.**
Str. 14/6—13/12/18.**G.**
Str. 2/9—30/11/21.**G.**
Str. 4/4—5/9/24.**G.**

BOILERS:
598.
598 ?/12/07.
2345 13/12/18.
598 30/11/21.

SHED:
Ipswich.

RENUMBERED:
7598 5/9/24.

CONDEMNED: 11/9/26.

7599

Sharp Stewart 3164.

To traffic 7/1884.

REPAIRS:
Str. 10/1—17/5/06.**G.**
Str. 31/1—13/6/19.**G.**
Str. 15/12/23—22/3/24.**G.**
Str. ?/?—?/9/26.**G.**
Str. 14/9—31/10/28.**G.**
Coal guard on tender.

BOILERS:
599.
599 17/5/06.
685 13/6/19.
2312 22/3/24.
2314 ?/9/26.
2318 31/10/28.

SHED:
Ipswich.

RENUMBERED:
7599 22/3/24.

CONDEMNED: 8/5/31.

7680

Stratford.

To traffic 2/1885.

REPAIRS:
Str. 26/5—3/11/05.**G.**
Str. 8/9—15/12/21.**G.**
Str. 21/4—15/9/23.**G.**
Str. ?/?—?/10/25.**G.**
Str. ?/4—?/5/28.**G.**
Coal guard on tender.
Str. 2—30/4/30.**G.**

BOILERS:
680.
680 3/11/05.
2340 15/12/21.
852 ?/10/25.
2304 ?/5/28.
2392 30/4/30.

SHEDS:
March.
Stratford ?/?/?.
March 29/9/27.

RENUMBERED:
7680 ?/10/25.

CONDEMNED: 24/6/32.

7681

Stratford.

To traffic 2/1885.

REPAIRS:
Str. 28/12/10—24/3/11.**G.**
Str. 7/6—5/10/21.**G.**
Str. 17/3—23/6/23.**G.**
Str. ?/?—?/7/25.**G.**
Str. ?/?—?/4/28.**G.**
Coal guard on tender.
Str. 23/4—16/5/30.**G.**

BOILERS:
681.
681 24/3/11.
809 5/10/21.
2308 ?/7/25.
2390 16/5/30.

SHEDS:
March.
Stratford ?/?/?.

7681 cont./
March 29/9/27.
Stratford 31/5/29.
March 8/8/29.

RENUMBERED:
7681 ?/7/25.

CONDEMNED: 8/10/32.

_____

7682

Stratford.

To traffic 2/1885.

REPAIRS:
???. ?/?—?/12/07.**G**.
Str. 15/3—10/8/21.**G**.
Str. 7/2—23/6/23.**G**.
Str. 8/5—19/8/25.**G**.
Str. ?/?—?/7/28.**G**.
Coal guard on tender.
Str. 15/7—15/8/30.**G**.

BOILERS:
682.
682 ?/12/07.
2368 10/8/21.
839 23/6/23.
2332 19/8/25.
818 15/8/30.

SHEDS:
March.
Stratford ?/?/?.
March 25/10/27.
Stratford 3/6/29.
March 23/9/29.

RENUMBERED:
7682 19/8/25.

CONDEMNED: 25/1/32.

_____

7683

Stratford.

To traffic 2/1885.

REPAIRS:
Str. 8/6—28/11/03.**G**.
Str. 17/5—8/10/18.**G**.
Dar. 2/7—29/10/23.**G**.
Str. 29/9—3/12/27.**G**.
Coal guard on tender.
Str. 25/10—20/11/29.**G**.

BOILERS:
683.
683 28/11/03.
891 8/10/18.

2376 29/10/23.
2329 3/12/27.
2306 20/11/29.

SHEDS:
March.
Cambridge ?/?/?.
Stratford 26/6/26.
March 24/11/29.

RENUMBERED:
 683ᴇ 29/10/23.
7683 ?/?

CONDEMNED: 7/11/31.

_____

7684

Stratford.

To traffic 2/1885.

REPAIRS:
Str. 1/3—15/7/10.**G**.
Str. 20/1—6/6/16.**G**.
Str. 23/3—31/8/22.**G**.
Str. 18/5—29/8/25.**G**.
Str. 19/11/27—24/1/28.**G**.
Coal guard on tender.
Str. 26/3—12/4/30.**G**.

BOILERS:
684.
684 15/7/10.
2327 6/6/16.
684 31/8/22.
610 29/8/25.
2313 24/1/28.
 39 12/4/30.

SHEDS:
Peterborough East *at* 1/22.
Stratford *at* 5/23.
Ipswich ?/?/?.
Stratford 24/1/28.

RENUMBERED:
7684 29/8/25.

CONDEMNED: 1/6/32.

_____

7685

Stratford.

To traffic 2/1885.

REPAIRS:
Str. 5/1—13/5/10.**G**.
Str. 3/9/18—5/2/19.**G**.
Str. 4/4—23/7/24.**G**.

BOILERS:
685.
685 13/5/10.
2352 5/2/19.
818 23/7/24.

SHEDS:
March.
Norwich ?/?/?.
Yarmouth 3/3/29.

RENUMBERED:
7685 23/7/24.

CONDEMNED: 23/10/29.

_____

7686

Stratford.

To traffic 2/1885.

REPAIRS:
Str. 12/7—4/10/10.**G**.
Str. 8/3—23/9/19.**G**.
Str. 31/3—6/7/23.**G**.
Str. 27/7—13/11/25.**G**.

BOILERS:
686.
686 4/10/10.
633 23/9/19.
684 6/7/23.
2363 13/11/25.

SHEDS:
Peterborough East.
Cambridge ?/?/?.

RENUMBERED:
7686 13/11/25.

CONDEMNED: 15/6/28.

_____

(7)688

Stratford.

To traffic 2/1885.

REPAIRS:
Str. 1/3—12/5/11.**G**.
Str. 11/11/19—2/3/20.**G**.

BOILERS:
688.
688 12/5/11.
614 2/3/20.

SHED:
Peterborough East.

CONDEMNED: 31/8/23.

7689

Stratford.

To traffic 2/1885.

REPAIRS:
Str. 16/3—29/6/11.**G**.
Str. 15/11/20—18/2/21.**G**.
Str. 24/2—2/7/26.**G**.
Str. ?/?—?/10/28.**G**.
Coal guard on tender.
Str. 13—24/4/31.**G**.
Str. 21/8—5/9/33.**G**.

BOILERS:
689.
689 29/6/11.
2361 18/2/21.
2382 2/7/26.
2336 24/4/31.
2372 5/9/33.

SHEDS:
March.
Ipswich *by* 3/24.
Norwich 26/4/34.
Ipswich 17/1/35.

RENUMBERED:
7689 ?/?

CONDEMNED: 30/6/36.

_____

7690

Stratford.

To traffic 11/1885.

REPAIRS:
Str. 8/4—16/8/10.**G**.
Str. 28/7/16—20/2/17.**G**.
Str. 27/4—28/7/22.**G**.
Str. 8/12/24—7/3/25.**G**.
Str. ?/?—?/4/26.**G**.
Str. ?/?—?/1/28.**G**.
Coal guard on tender.
Str. 27/3—12/4/30.**G**.
Str. 11—28/10/32.**G**.
Str. 26/2—9/3/36.**G**.

BOILERS:
690.
690 16/8/10.
684 20/2/17.
826 28/7/22.
2380 ?/4/26.
2370 12/4/30.
2304 28/10/32.
2358 9/3/36.

SHEDS:
Colchester.

7690 cont./
King's Lynn 30/10/34.
March 10/6/36.

RENUMBERED:
7690 7/3/25.

*SOLD: to Baird & Co. Ltd.,
Gartsherrie, 7/6/38.
Cow. 3/10—27/12/45.***G.**
Changed Boiler.

7691

Stratford.

To traffic 11/1885.

REPAIRS:
Str. 29/10/10—9/1/11.**G.**
Str. 24/10/19—10/2/20.**G.**
Str. ?/?—?/8/24.**G.**
Str. 22/11/26—22/1/27.**G.**

BOILERS:
691.
691 9/1/11.
613 10/2/20.
2312 22/1/27.

SHED:
Colchester.

RENUMBERED:
7691 ?/8/24.

CONDEMNED: 16/3/29.

7692

Stratford.

To traffic 12/1885.

REPAIRS:
Str. 21/6—6/9/10.**G.**
Str. 1/3—11/6/18.**G.**
Str. 25/11/21—16/3/22.**G.**
Str. 24/12/26—5/2/27.**G.**

BOILERS:
692.
692 6/9/10.
2339 11/6/18.
849 16/3/22.
2300 5/2/27.

SHED:
Colchester.

RENUMBERED:
7692 *by* 25/2/25.

CONDEMNED: 20/4/29.

7693

Stratford.

To traffic 12/1885.

REPAIRS:
Str. 14/9/10—3/1/11.**G.**
Records missing.
Str. 24/2—16/7/26.**G.**

BOILERS:
693.
693 3/1/11.
2357 16/7/26.

SHED:
Colchester.

RENUMBERED:
7693 *by* 25/2/25.

CONDEMNED: 14/7/28.

7694

Stratford.

To traffic 1/1886.

REPAIRS:
Str. 21/12/09—10/5/10.**G.**
Str. 12/7—3/12/18.**G.**
???. 8/4—26/8/21.**G.**
Records missing.
Str. ?/?—?/4/29.**G.**
Coal guard on tender.

BOILERS:
694.
694 10/5/10.
2341 3/12/18.
2362 ?/4/29.

SHEDS:
Ipswich.
Parkeston 20/2/28.
Ipswich 16/5/28.
Norwich 30/4/29.
Yarmouth 3/8/30.
Norwich 5/4/31.

RENUMBERED:
7694 ?/?

CONDEMNED: 9/10/31.

7696

Stratford.

To traffic 12/1885.

REPAIRS:
Str. 25/3—28/6/11.**G.**
Str. 8/8/19—15/1/20.**G.**
In works 31/5/24.
Str. 11/2—28/5/26.**G.**
Str. 13/7—2/10/28.**G.**
Coal guard on tender.
Str. 17/7—20/8/30.**G.**
Str. 4—14/10/32.**G.**

BOILERS:
696.
696 28/6/11.
861 15/1/20.
2369 28/5/26.
690 2/10/28.
2358 20/8/30.
2386 14/10/32.

SHEDS:
Stratford.
Ipswich ?/?/?.
Stratford 24/9/27.
March 21/11/29.
New England 23/10/33.
Grantham 14/2/36.
New England 27/4/36.

RENUMBERED:
7696 31/5/24.

CONDEMNED: 18/3/38.

7697

Stratford.

To traffic 1/1886.

REPAIRS:
Str. 17/11/11—19/4/12.**G.**
Str. 13/6—30/10/17.**G.**
Str. 30/7—25/9/20.**G.**
Str. ?/?—?/5/25.**G.**
Str. ?/?—?/11/27.**G.**
Coal guard on tender.

BOILERS:
697.
697 19/4/12.
879 30/10/17.

2308 25/9/20.
611 ?/5/25.

SHED:
Stratford.

RENUMBERED:
7697 ?/5/25.

CONDEMNED: 25/10/29.

7698

Stratford.

To traffic 2/1886.

REPAIRS:
Str. 31/8—7/11/11.**G.**
Str. 14/8—27/12/16.**G.**
Str. 30/4—29/7/18.**G.**
Str. 9/8—24/11/23.**G.**
Str. ?/?—?/11/25.**G.**
Str. ?/?—?/5/28.**G.**
Coal guard on tender.
Str. 23/9—10/10/30.**G.**
Str. 10—25/8/33.**G.**
Frames altered.

BOILERS:
698.
698 7/11/11.
2330 27/12/16.
851 29/7/18.
2338 24/11/23.
684 ?/11/25.
2364 10/10/30.
2562 25/8/33.

SHEDS:
Southend.
Stratford ?/?/?.
Southend 3/5/30.
Stratford *by* 5/32.
Cambridge 10/11/34.
King's Lynn 23/2/35.

RENUMBERED:
7698 ?/11/25.

CONDEMNED: 31/10/36.

WORKS CODES:- Cam - Cambridge shed. Dar - Darlington. Don - Doncaster. Ips - Ipwich shed. Nor - Norwich shed. Pbo - Peterborough East shed. Str - Stratford.
REPAIR CODES:- C/H - Casual Heavy. C/L - Casual Light. G - General. H- Heavy. H/I - Heavy Intermediate. L - Light. L/I - Light Intermediate. N/C - Non-Classified.

23

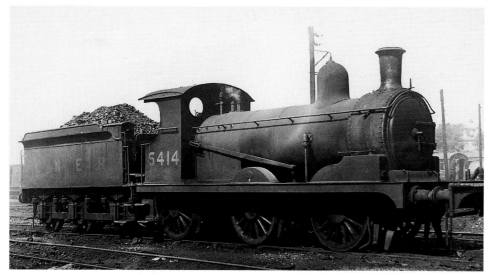

In 1940 it was thought that enemy action might cause the J15's to have to work over London Transport lines so a number were fitted with the shorter chimney used by E4 and F3 classes, which cut the chimney height to 12ft 3½ins. No.5414 still had one of those at its 7th November 1949 withdrawal, but Nos.65388 and 65440 carried them to their respective 22nd May 1959 and 10th October 1960 withdrawals (*see* page 90, centre).

(above) During May 1960, Norwich shed found two stovepipes of the original Great Eastern design which they restored to two of their allocation one of which was 65469. Stratford.

The other orthodox stovepipe was first put on No.65471 but that engine was withdrawn on 17th June 1960 and the chimney passed to No.65462 which had it to its 16th September 1962 withdrawal, and ultimately as preserved.

All originally had Ramsbottom safety valves in a casing and with the whistle on the same mounting.

After Grouping the LNER standardised on Ross 'pop' safety valves and at first put them on Ramsbottom type mountings. Stratford, 26th March 1937.

Subsequently the Ross 'pops' were mounted directly on to the firebox and the whistle was put on a separate pipe between the safety valves and the front of the cab. Stratford, 26th March 1937.

All originally had a wooden cab roof 7ft 6⅞ins across the edges and with 11ft 3ins height from the rail, the roof radius being 12ft 6ins.

7699

Stratford.

To traffic 3/1886.

REPAIRS:
Str. 27/1—14/6/12.**G.**
Str. 14/11/19—21/2/20.**G.**
Str. ?/?—?/5/23.**G.**
Str. 20/3—6/6/24.**G.**
Str. ?/?—?/11/28.**G.**
Coal guard on tender.
Str. 9—26/6/31.**G.**

BOILERS:
699.
699 14/6/12.
877 21/2/20.
600 ?/5/23.
2383 26/6/31.

SHEDS:
Stratford.
March 23/7/31.
Stratford 21/9/31.

RENUMBERED:
7699 6/6/24.

CONDEMNED: 25/7/34.

7609

Stratford.

To traffic 4/1886.

REPAIRS:
Str. 23/6—15/9/10.**G.**
Str. 5/9/19—4/2/20.**G.**
Str. 3/8/26—14/1/27.**G.**
Str. ?/?—?/9/29.**G.**
Coal guard on tender.
Str. 8—25/8/32.**G.**
Frames altered.

BOILERS:
800.
609 15/9/10.
595 14/1/27.
535 ?/9/29.
2784 25/8/32.

SHEDS:
Norwich.
Ipswich ?/?/?.

RENUMBERED:
 609 from **800** 1/92.
7609 ?/?

CONDEMNED: 17/10/35.

7801

Stratford.

To traffic 4/1886.

REPAIRS:
Str. 21/8—18/10/12.**G.**
Str. 17/6—21/10/21.**G.**
Str. 3/6—31/8/27.**G.**
Str. 12—26/9/29.**G.**
Coal guard on tender.
Str. 11—28/11/31.**G.**

BOILERS:
801.
801 18/10/12.
620 21/10/21.
802 31/8/27.
2375 26/9/29.
2354 28/11/31.

SHED:
King's Lynn.

RENUMBERED:
7801 *by* 23/2/26.

CONDEMNED: 24/1/35.

7802

Stratford.

To traffic 5/1886.

REPAIRS:
Str. 15/10/09—24/2/10.**G.**
Str. 24/12/20—9/3/21.**G.**
Records missing.

BOILERS:
 802.
 802 24/2/10.
2362 9/3/21.

SHED:
King's Lynn.

RENUMBERED:
Still **802** 14/6/24.
7802 ?/?

CONDEMNED: 19/1/29.

7803

Stratford.

To traffic 5/1886.

REPAIRS:
Str. 21/3—10/7/12.**G.**

Str. 24/1—21/4/22.**G.**
Str. 20—31/12/27.**G.**
Coal guard on tender.
Str. 9/7—8/8/30.**G.**
Str. 24/8—8/9/32.**G.**

BOILERS:
 803.
 803 10/7/12.
2372 21/4/22.
2356 31/12/27.
2326 8/8/30.
2353 8/9/32.

SHEDS:
March.
Ipswich ?/?/?.
Stratford 26/9/27.
Norwich 4/1/29.

RENUMBERED:
7803 ?/?

CONDEMNED: 12/12/35.

7805

Stratford.

To traffic 7/1886.

REPAIRS:
Str. ?/?—?/6/08.**G.**
Str. 20/7—10/12/18.**G.**
Str. 27/8—29/11/23.**G.**
Str. 17/10/25—29/1/26.**G.**

BOILERS:
 805.
 805 ?/6/08.
2346 10/12/18.
 124 29/11/23.

SHED:
Cambridge.

RENUMBERED:
7805 29/1/26.

CONDEMNED: 27/4/28.

7806

Stratford.

To traffic 7/1886.

REPAIRS:
Str. ?/?—?/12/00.**G.**
Str. 21/7—27/10/16.**G.**
Cam. 21/8—1/10/23.**H.**
Str. 28/6—6/11/24.**G.**
Str. 12/5—18/8/27.**G.**

Str. 24/1—1/3/30.**G.**
Coal guard on tender.
Str. 5/7—5/8/32.**G.**
Frames altered.
Str. 23/12/35—31/1/36.**G.**
New steel cab roof.
Str. 18/9/39. *Not repaired.*

BOILERS:
 806.
 806 ?/12/00.
2328 27/10/16.
2385 1/3/30.
2779 5/8/32.
2792 31/1/36.

SHEDS:
Cambridge.
March 25/9/32.
Norwich 18/9/36.
Lowestoft 30/3/37.
Norwich 8/9/39.

RENUMBERED:
7806 6/11/24.

CONDEMNED: 31/10/39.
Cut up at Stratford.

7807

Stratford.

To traffic 7/1886.

REPAIRS:
Str. 29/5/08—7/1/09.**G.**
Str. 6—25/1/24.**G.**
Str. 16/8—31/12/26.**G.**

BOILERS:
 807.
 807 7/1/09.
2366 25/1/24.
2335 31/2/26.

SHED:
Norwich.

RENUMBERED:
7807 ?/?

CONDEMNED: 16/3/29.

7809

Stratford.

To traffic 8/1886.

REPAIRS:
Str. 15/6—11/8/11.**G.**
Str. 28/2—11/6/21.**G.**

7809 cont./
Records missing.
Str. 21/1—28/4/28.**G.**
Coal guard on tender.
Str. 16—26/9/30.**G.**
Str. 16—31/8/33.**G.**
Frames altered.

BOILERS:
 809.
 809 11/8/11.
 2365 11/6/21.
 2322 28/4/28.
 2332 26/9/30.
 3308 31/8/33.

SHEDS:
Norwich.
Ipswich 15/9/27.
Norwich 28/4/28.

RENUMBERED:
7809 ?/?

CONDEMNED: 6/8/36.

_____

7810

Stratford.

To traffic 11/1886.

REPAIRS:
Str. 16/12/11—15/5/12.**G.**
Str. 27/6/19—22/1/20.**G.**
Records missing.
Str. ?/?—?/10/26.**G.**

BOILERS:
 810.
 810 15/5/12.
 2301 22/1/20.
 2303 ?/10/26.

SHED:
Norwich.

RENUMBERED:
7810 ?/?

CONDEMNED: 24/1/29.

_____

7812

Stratford.

To traffic 12/1886.

REPAIRS:
Str. 18/4—21/9/99.**G.**
Str. 20/4—21/7/16.**G.**
Str. 5/4—13/8/24.**G.**

BOILERS:
 812.
 812 21/9/99.
 2326 21/7/16.
 2345 13/4/24.

SHEDS:
Lowestoft.
Norwich ?/?/?.

RENUMBERED:
7812 13/8/24.

CONDEMNED: 16/2/29.

_____

7813

Stratford.

To traffic 12/1886.

REPAIRS:
Str. ?/?—?/6/07.**G.**
Str. 28/4—23/7/14.**G.**
Str. 23/11/22—7/3/23.**G.**
Str. 12/5—14/8/25.**G.**
Str. 18/7—31/10/27.**G.**
Str. 29/3—9/5/30.**G.**
Coal guard on tender.
Str. 21/11—28/12/32.**G.**
Str. 6/6—24/8/36.**G.**
Str. 2/2—20/4/40.**G.**
Str. 18/3—30/4/43.**G.**
Str. 26/8—13/9/45.**G.**
Frames altered.
Str. 5/11—13/12/47.**G.**

BOILERS:
 813.
 813 ?/6/07.
 2306 23/7/14.
 2316 7/3/23.
 2328 9/5/30.
 2370 28/12/32.
 2387 24/8/36.
 2392 30/4/43.
 3373 13/9/45.
 2796 13/12/47.

SHEDS:
Norwich.
March 3/10/24.
Norwich 9/12/24.
New England 6/9/37.
Cambridge 5/3/41.

RENUMBERED:
7813 14/8/25.
5350 11/8/46.

CONDEMNED: 26/2/51.
Cut up at Stratford.

_____

7814

Stratford.

To traffic 12/1886.

REPAIRS:
Str. ?/?—?/6/06.**G.**
Str. 21/9—30/12/22.**G.**
Nor. ?/?—?/8/24.**H.**
Str. ?/?—?/8/29.**G.**
Coal guard on tender.
Str. 14/7—4/8/32.**G.**
Frames altered.
Str. 4—20/9/35.**G.**

BOILERS:
 814.
 814 ?/6/06.
 2325 30/12/22.
 2367 ?/8/29.
 2529 4/8/32.
 2561 20/9/35.

SHEDS:
Yarmouth.
Norwich 5/7/29.
Yarmouth 4/10/31.
Norwich 20/12/31.
Lowestoft 25/9/32.
Norwich 19/7/35.

RENUMBERED:
7814 ?/8/24.

CONDEMNED: 17/8/38.

_____

7815

Stratford.

To traffic 1/1887.

REPAIRS:
Str. 24/7—14/11/13.**G.**
Str. 20/3—26/7/23.**G.**
Str. 6/3—13/8/26.**G.**
Str. 27/8—9/10/28.**G.**
Coal guard on tender.
Str. 13/11—5/12/30.**G.**
Str. 7—24/4/33.**G.**

BOILERS:
 815.
 815 14/11/13.
 2368 26/7/23.
 826 13/8/26.
 2311 9/10/28.
 2387 5/12/30.
 825 24/4/33.

SHEDS:
Norwich.

Ipswich 3/11/28.
Parkeston 19/6/33.

RENUMBERED:
7815 13/8/26.

CONDEMNED: 4/6/36.

_____

7816

Stratford.

To traffic 1/1887.

REPAIRS:
Str. ?/?—?/6/07.**G.**
Str. 5/4—30/8/24.**G.**

BOILERS:
816.
816 ?/6/07.
685 30/8/24.

SHED:
Norwich.

RENUMBERED:
7816 30/8/24.

CONDEMNED: 3/1/30.

_____

7817

Stratford.

To traffic 2/1887.

REPAIRS:
Str. ?/?—?/12/98.**G.**
Str. 27/3—13/8/14.**G.**
Str. 12/2—7/5/24.**G.**
Str. ?/?—?/2/27.**G.**
Coal guard on tender.
Str. ?/?—?/6/29.**G.**
Str. 9—21/11/31.**G.**

BOILERS:
 817.
 817 ?/12/98.
 2302 13/8/14.
 2344 7/5/24.
 2335 ?/6/29.
 2314 21/11/31.

SHEDS:
Norwich.
Cambridge 6/10/25.
Norwich 12/12/25.
Yarmouth 5/7/29.
Norwich 5/4/31.
Yarmouth 4/9/33.
Norwich 10/11/33.
King's Lynn 16/11/33.

7817 cont./
RENUMBERED:
7817 7/5/24.

CONDEMNED: 13/3/36.

_____

7818

Stratford.

To traffic 2/1887.

REPAIRS:
Str. 21/1—8/6/10.**G.**
Str. 26/5—16/9/17.**G.**
Str. 13/3—23/5/24.**G.**
Str. 23/12/26—12/3/27.**G.**
Str. ?/?—?/8/29.**G.**
Coal guard on tender.
Str. 25/7—16/8/32.**G.**
Frames altered.
Str. 30/9—16/10/35.**G.**

BOILERS:
818.
818 8/6/10.
834 16/9/17.
698 23/5/24.
805 12/3/27.
534 ?/8/29.
2781 16/8/32.
2729 16/10/35.

SHEDS:
Norwich.
Cambridge 11/10/37.
Norwich 8/1/38.

RENUMBERED:
7818 23/5/24.

CONDEMNED: 18/11/38.

_____

7819

Stratford.

To traffic 2/1887.

REPAIRS:
Str. 20/2—4/5/11.**G.**
Str. 7/1—8/4/21.**G.**
Str. 7/11/27—3/2/28.**G.**
Coal guard on tender.
Str. 5—26/6/30.**G.**
Str. 11—26/8/32.**G.**
Frames altered.
Str. 29/10—14/11/35.**G.**

BOILERS:
819.
819 4/5/11.
629 8/4/21.

2371 3/2/28.
2377 26/6/30.
2783 26/8/32.
2791 14/11/35.

SHEDS:
Norwich.
Stratford 4/2/28.
Cambridge 25/10/37.
Stratford 7/1/38.

RENUMBERED:
Still **819** *at* 30/10/24.
7819 ?/?

CONDEMNED: 5/4/38.

_____

7820

Stratford.

To traffic 9/1887.

REPAIRS:
Str. ?/?—?/12/99.**G.**
Str. 21/7—31/10/16.**G.**
Str. 5/1—24/3/23.**G.**
Str. 23/7—4/11/25.**G.**

BOILERS:
820.
820 ?/12/99.
2329 31/10/16.
2331 24/3/23.
690 4/11/25.

SHEDS:
Norwich.
Cambridge ?/?/?.
Norwich 5/10/27.

RENUMBERED:
7820 4/10/25.

CONDEMNED: 8/7/28.

_____

7821

Stratford.

To traffic 9/1887.

REPAIRS:
Str. 27/6—21/10/13.**G.**
Str. 17/3—11/9/23.**G.**
Str. 28/9—21/12/25.**G.**
Str. 23/11/27—17/2/28.**G.**
Coal guard on tender.
Str. 4/2—22/3/30.**G.**
Str. 22/8—16/9/32.**G.**
Str. 13/8—6/9/35.**G.**
Str. 17/7—24/8/38.**G.**
Str. 7/10—14/11/41.**G.**

Str. 6/2—24/3/44.**G.**
Str. 24/3—14/5/46.**G.**

BOILERS:
821.
821 21/10/13.
2349 21/12/25.
2386 22/3/30.
2385 16/9/32.
2396 6/9/35.
2323 24/8/38.
2388 14/11/41.
2379 24/3/44.

SHEDS:
Peterborough East.
March 1/9/29.
Ipswich 22/3/30.
Colchester 5/4/30.
Norwich 31/10/32.
Lowestoft 30/3/37.
Norwich 26/3/44.
Lowestoft 23/4/44.

RENUMBERED:
821ᴇ 11/9/23.
7821 21/12/25.
5351 10/5/46.

CONDEMNED: 31/5/49.
Cut up at Stratford.

_____

7823

Stratford.

To traffic 9/1887.

REPAIRS:
Str. 11/2—28/7/02.**G.**
Str. 3/12/14—6/3/15.**G.**
Str. 7/12/20—8/3/21.**G.**
Str. 21/5—24/9/25.**G.**
Str. 22/4—12/8/27.**G.**
Str. ?/?—?/5/29.**G.**
Coal guard on tender.
Str. 9—24/9/31.**G.**
Str. 26/4—8/5/34.**G.**

BOILERS:
823.
823 28/7/02.
2313 6/3/15.
2363 8/3/21.
839 24/9/25.
696 12/8/27.
693 ?/5/29.
2361 24/9/31.
2356 8/5/34.

SHEDS:
Stratford.
Ipswich 21/10/27.
Parkeston 20/2/28.

Ipswich 1/5/28.
New England 26/5/34.
Cambridge 23/11/34.
March 26/1/35.
New England 17/10/35.

RENUMBERED:
7823 24/9/25.

CONDEMNED: 31/5/37.

_____

7824

Stratford.

To traffic 9/1887.

REPAIRS:
Str. ?/?—?/12/01.**G.**
Str. 8/5—14/10/15.**G.**
Str. 11/2—29/4/24.**G.**
Str. 9—24/8/29.**G.**
Coal guard on tender.
Str. 5—22/9/32.**G.**

BOILERS:
824.
824 ?/12/01.
123 14/10/15.
2319 29/4/24.
2346 24/8/29.
2391 22/9/32.

SHEDS:
Norwich.
Lowestoft 8/7/33.
Norwich 28/12/35.

RENUMBERED:
7824 29/4/24.

CONDEMNED: 23/1/36.

_____

7825

Stratford.

To traffic 9/1887.

REPAIRS:
Str. 21/8/13—27/1/14.**G.**
Str. 31/1—20/4/20.**G.**
Str. 23/9—31/12/25.**G.**
Str. ?/?—?/9/28.**G.**
Coal guard on tender.
Str. 28/4—15/5/31.**G.**
Str. 24/8—14/9/33.**G.**
Str. 18—29/5/36.**G.**
Str. ?/?—?/5/40.**G.**
Str. ?/?—?/8/43.**G.**
Str. 16/6—14/7/45.**G.**

7825 cont./
BOILERS:
 825.
 825 27/1/14.
 688 20/4/20.
 626 31/12/25.
 2363 15/5/31.
 2364 14/9/33.
 2380 29/5/36.
 2390 ?/5/40.
 2387 ?/8/43.
 2372 14/7/45.

SHEDS:
Cambridge.
Norwich 24/3/37.
Lowestoft 16/1/44.
Norwich 1/6/47.
Lowestoft 15/6/47.

RENUMBERED:
7825 31/12/25.
5352 10/11/46.

CONDEMNED: 29/5/48.
Cut up at Stratford.

_____

7826

Stratford.

To traffic 9/1887.

REPAIRS:
Str. 29/8—31/10/12.**G**.
Str. 9/1—28/4/22.**G**.
Str. 1/4—2/6/27.**G**.
Coal guard on tender.

BOILERS:
 826.
 826 31/10/12.
2371 28/4/22.
2370 2/6/27.

SHED:
Cambridge.

RENUMBERED:
7826 ?/?

CONDEMNED: 21/9/29.

_____

7827

Stratford.

To traffic 9/1887.

REPAIRS:
Str. ?/?—?/12/04.**G**.
Str. 22/4—22/7/22.**G**.
Str. 17/12/26—18/2/27.**G**.

BOILERS:
 827.
 827 ?/12/04.
2375 22/7/22.
 697 18/2/27.

SHED:
Peterborough East.

RENUMBERED:
Still **827** at 31/5/24.
7827 ?/?

CONDEMNED: 21/2/29.

_____

7828

Stratford.

To traffic 9/1887.

REPAIRS:
Str. 5/6—29/8/12.**G**.
Nor. 8/5—3/8/22.**H**.
Str. 5/8/26—27/1/27.**G**.
Str. 1/6—19/7/29.**G**.
Coal guard on tender.
Str. 4—22/1/32.**G**.
Str. 20/8—13/9/35.**G**.
Str. 16/9—4/11/38.**G**.
Str. 24/9—17/10/42.**G**.
Frames altered.
Str. 12/11—2/12/44.**G**.
Str. 5—24/1/46.**L**.
Str. 6/4—19/5/47.**G**.

BOILERS:
 828.
 828 29/8/12.
2341 19/7/29.
2375 22/1/32.
2374 13/9/35.
3334 17/10/42.
2564 2/12/44.
3350 19/5/47.

SHEDS:
Norwich.
Yarmouth 3/3/29.
Norwich 25/3/29.
Yarmouth ?/?/?.
Norwich 27/12/31.
Lowestoft 10/10/48.
Norwich 13/3/49.
Ipswich 5/6/49.

RENUMBERED:
7828 ?/?
5353 20/10/46.

CONDEMNED: 5/12/49.
Cut up at Stratford.

_____

7829

Stratford.

To traffic 9/1887.

REPAIRS:
Str. 15/3—15/7/10.**G**.
Str. 7/12/20—28/2/21.**G**.
Str. 6/1—5/4/28.**G**.
Coal guard on tender.
Str. 3—19/9/30.**G**.
Str. 18—29/9/33.**G**.

BOILERS:
 829.
 829 15/7/10.
2364 28/2/21.
2359 5/4/28.
2371 19/9/30.
2336 29/9/33.

SHED:
Norwich.

RENUMBERED:
Still **829** at 1/9/24.
7829 - grey - in 1926.

CONDEMNED: 26/8/36.

_____

7527

Stratford.

To traffic 10/1887.

REPAIRS:
Str. ?/?—?/12/01.**G**.
Str. 1/10—1/12/14.**G**.
Str. 25/5—28/9/22.**G**.
Str. 1/9—12/12/24.**G**.
Str. 16/5—27/7/27.**G**.
Str. 7/6—19/7/29.**G**.
Coal guard on tender.
Str. 29/7—5/9/31.**G**.
Str. 12/5—17/7/34.**G**.
Str. 5—30/10/37.**G**.
Str. 9/12/41—3/1/42.**G**.
Str. 5/9—6/10/44.**G**.
Str. 15/10—22/11/47.**G**.

BOILERS:
 527.
 527 ?/12/01.
2309 1/12/14.
 802 28/9/22.
 528 12/12/24.
2345 19/7/29.
2393 5/9/31.
2361 17/7/34.
2372 30/10/37.
2396 3/1/42.
2397 6/10/44.

2387 22/11/47.

SHEDS:
Cambridge.
March 28/10/28.
Cambridge 23/2/35.
Ipswich 30/9/35.
Stratford 1/4/39.
Cambridge 10/11/39.
Stratford 16/12/40.
Cambridge 6/11/41.
Bury St Edmunds 27/11/46.
Stratford 6/12/46.
Parkeston 1/1/50.

RENUMBERED:
7527 12/12/24.
5354 23/6/46.

CONDEMNED: 26/2/51.
Cut up at Stratford.

_____

7528

Stratford.

To traffic 10/1887.

REPAIRS:
Str. 30/11/07—27/3/08.**G**.
Str. 8/11/18—22/5/19.**G**.
Str. 11—17/6/21.**N/C**.
Liquid fuel fitted.
Str. 15/12/24—11/3/25.**G**.
Str. ?/?—?/1/28.**G**.
Coal guard on tender.

BOILERS:
 528.
 528 27/3/08.
2330 22/5/19.
 877 11/3/25.

SHEDS:
Lincoln.
Cambridge ?/?/?.
March 28/10/28.

RENUMBERED:
7528 11/3/25.

CONDEMNED: 10/2/30.

_____

7529

Stratford.

To traffic 11/1887.

REPAIRS:
Str. ?/?—?/12/02.**G**.
Str. 6/10/15—3/3/16.**G**.
Str. 1/2—6/6/23.**G**.

Beginning in 1933 a new steel cab roof was fitted. This was only 7ft 4ins across the edges, but the radius was cut to 8ft 0ins in the middle, sharpening to 3ft 3ins. at each side, and the height from rail became 11ft 5³/₄ins. Many still had a wooden roof at withdrawal but the one hundred and thirty survivors at 1939 all then had the steel roof.

For working on the Colne Valley line (which was devoid of turntables), five J15's were fitted with a side window cab and a back cab. They were: 7941 (12th July 1934), 7523 (20th July 1934), 7888 (17th August 1934), 7911 (27th September 1934), and 7512 (11th January 1935). They were also fitted with vacuum ejector equipment, carriage heating apparatus, and balanced wheels.

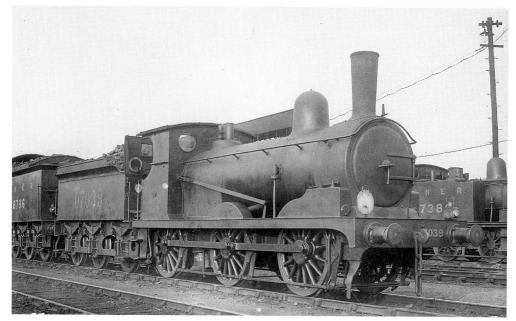

There were also some earlier and widely varied shed fittings of weatherboards for tender-first workings. No.07039 had this effort by 1928, for jobs in the Ipswich area. Stratford shed.

No.7875 working from Stratford acquired this weatherboard by 1927.

No.7859 at Peterborough East shed had this back cab by 1932. It also had extra crew protection from the flexible connection to the cab.

7529 cont./
Str. 17/10/25—23/1/26.**G**.
Str. ?/?—?/5/28.**G**.
Coal guard on tender.
Str. 20/5—13/6/30.**G**.

BOILERS:
529.
529 ?/12/02.
2319 3/3/16.
858 6/6/23.
2338 23/1/26.
2379 13/6/30.

SHEDS:
Cambridge.
March 28/10/28.

RENUMBERED:
7529 23/1/26.

CONDEMNED: 5/12/31.

_____

7530

Stratford.

To traffic 11/1887.

REPAIRS:
Str. 4/3—24/10/01.**G**.
Str. 23/12/15—20/4/16.**G**.
Fitted with tender 1011.
Cam. 10/7—10/9/23.**H**.
Str. 5/6—22/8/24.**G**.
Str. 11/2—28/4/27.**G**.
Str. 29/8—4/10/29.**G**.
Coal guard on tender.
Str. 12/5—21/6/32.**G**.
Frames altered.
Str. 1/7—15/8/35.**G**.
Str. 5/9—13/10/38.**G**.
Str. 10/6—27/7/42.**G**.
Str. 15/10—9/11/44.**G**.
Str. 21/9—13/11/47.**G**.

BOILERS:
530.
530 24/10/01.
2321 20/4/16.
2310 22/8/24.
2352 4/10/29.
2778 21/6/32.
2548 15/8/35.
3306 13/10/38.
3330 27/7/42.
2769 9/11/44.
3326 13/11/47.

SHEDS:
Cambridge.
King's Lynn 1/11/31.
March 4/3/33.
Norwich 14/4/33.

Yarmouth 5/10/35.
Norwich 17/12/35.
Lowestoft 29/3/36.
Norwich 6/11/38.
Lowestoft 19/9/43.

RENUMBERED:
7530 22/8/24.
5355 1/12/46.

CONDEMNED: 23/4/51.
Cut up at Stratford.

_____

7531

Stratford.

To traffic 11/1887.

REPAIRS:
Str. 19/2—21/10/01.**G**.
Str. 11/11/14—9/2/15.**G**.
Records missing.
Str. 31/10/25—5/2/26.**G**.

BOILERS:
531.
531 21/10/01.
2311 9/2/15.
2318 5/2/26.

SHED:
Cambridge.

RENUMBERED:
7531 ?/?

CONDEMNED: 20/8/28.

_____

7532

Stratford.

To traffic 1/1888.

REPAIRS:
Str. ?/?—12/02.**G**.
Str. 10/10/14—19/2/15.**G**.
Str. 10/11/23—1/2/24.**G**.
???. 12/10/25—?/?/?.**?**.
Str. 22/5—7/9/28.**G**.
Coal guard on tender.
Str. 15/7—5/9/30.**G**.
Str. 19/1—16/2/33.**G**.
Str. 16/12/35—21/1/36.**G**.
Str. 27/9—26/10/39.**G**.
Frames altered.
Str. 19/9—30/10/43.**G**.
Str. 18/3—13/4/45.**G**.
Str. 16/11—19/12/47.**G**.
Str. 8—26/8/50.**G**.
Str. 24/12/51—19/1/52.**C/H**.
Str. 17/11—13/12/52.**G**.

Str. 21/3/57. *Not repaired.*

BOILERS:
532.
532 ?/12/02.
2312 19/2/15.
2336 1/2/24.
2313 5/9/30.
2381 16/2/33.
2378 21/1/36.
2381 26/10/39.
3318 30/10/43.
3367 13/4/45.
3327 19/12/47.
3394 26/8/50.
23541 19/1/52.
23570 13/12/52.

SHEDS:
Cambridge.
Stratford 11/6/27.
Cambridge 1/10/27.
March 28/12/27.
Peterborough East 26/6/36.
New England 30/4/39.
Cambridge 3/3/41.
Bury St Edmunds 26/10/41.
Cambridge 8/2/42.
March 9/12/51.

RENUMBERED:
7532 ?/10/25.
5356 23/6/46.
65356 26/8/50.

CONDEMNED: 8/4/57.
Cut up at Stratford.

_____

7533

Stratford.

To traffic 1/1888.

REPAIRS:
Str. 30/4—7/12/97.**G**.
Str. 7/7—7/10/14.**G**.
Str. 9—15/6/21.**N/C**.
Liquid fuel fitted.
Str. 2/11/25—12/2/26.**G**.

BOILERS:
533.
533 7/12/97.
2307 7/10/14.
821 12/2/26.

SHEDS:
March.
Kings Lynn ?/?/?.

RENUMBERED:
7533 ?/?

CONDEMNED: 5/5/28.

_____

7534

Stratford.

To traffic 1/1888.

REPAIRS:
Str. 15/1—25/8/08.**G**.
Str. 26/5—5/12/19.**G**.
Str. 4/4—22/7/24.**G**.

BOILERS:
534.
534 25/8/08.
840 22/7/24.

SHED:
Stratford.

RENUMBERED:
7534 22/7/24.

CONDEMNED: 18/5/29.

_____

7535

Stratford.

To traffic 1/1888.

REPAIRS:
Str. 7/2—19/6/12.**G**.
Str. 7/12/17—17/5/18.**G**.
Records missing.
Str. ?/?—?/4/24.**G**.
Records missing.
Str. 21/2—15/3/30.**G**.
Coal guard on tender.
Str. 27/2—10/3/33.**G**.

BOILERS:
535.
535 19/6/12.
886 17/5/18.
2378 ?/4/24.
2339 15/3/30.
2351 10/3/33.

SHEDS:
Cambridge.
Norwich 5/4/27.
Lowestoft *at* 5/32.
Norwich 23/10/32.

RENUMBERED:
7535 ?/4/24.

CONDEMNED: 10/3/36.

_____

(7)536

Stratford.

To traffic 1/1888.

REPAIRS:
Str. 29/6—30/11/00.**G.**
Str. 27/1—17/5/16.**G.**

BOILERS:
536.
536 30/11/00.
2322 17/5/16.

SHED:
Cambridge.

CONDEMNED: 31/8/23.

---

(7)537

Stratford.

To traffic 10/1888.

REPAIRS:
Str. ?/?—?/6/02.**G.**
Str. 20/1—6/5/15**G.**
Str. 19/11/20—9/2/21.**G.**

BOILERS:
537.
537 ?/6/02.
2314 6/5/15.
690 9/2/21.

SHED:
Ipswich.

CONDEMNED: 31/8/23.

7538

Stratford.

To traffic 10/1888.

REPAIRS:
Str. 25/1—13/8/07.**G.**
Str. 17/8—28/12/17.**G.**
Str. 5/11/20—4/2/21.**G.**
Str. 29/2—4/6/24.**G.**
Str. ?/12/26—?/2/27.**G.**
Coal guard on tender.
Str. ?/?—?/2/29.**G.**
Str. 29/6—15/7/31.**G.**
Str. 10—31/10/33.**G.**
Str. 6—23/4/36.**G.**

BOILERS:
538.
538 13/8/07.

697 28/12/17.
2310 4/2/21.
2343 4/6/24.
2347 ?/2/29.
2388 15/7/31.
2311 31/10/33.
2391 23/4/36.

SHED:
Ipswich.

RENUMBERED:
7538 4/6/24.

CONDEMNED: 5/12/38.

7539

Stratford.

To traffic 10/1888.

REPAIRS:
Str. 29/10/01—19/2/02.**G.**
Str. 5/1—11/4/17.**G.**
Str. 3/11/21—17/2/22.**G.**
Str. 20/3—14/6/24.**G.**
Str. 24/12/26—12/2/27.**G.**
Str. ?/?—?/12/28.**G.**
Str. 1—17/7/31.**G.**
Coal guard on tender.
Str. 5—22/9/33.**G.**

BOILERS:
539.
539 19/2/02.
630 11/4/17.
2345 17/2/22.
846 14/6/24.
2353 12/2/27.
815 ?/12/28.
2382 17/7/31.
2331 22/9/33.

SHEDS:
Colchester.
Ipswich *at* 3/32.

RENUMBERED:
7539 14/6/24.

CONDEMNED: 23/6/36.

7540

Stratford.

To traffic 10/1888.

REPAIRS:
Str. 5/12/03—23/7/04.**G.**
Str. 16/11/21—24/3/22.**G.**
Str. 19/9—10/12/24.**G.**

Str. 12/5—18/8/27.**G.**
Str. 13/12/29—1/2/30.**G.**
Coal guard on tender.
Str. 4/6—4/7/32.**G.**
Str. 17/10—15/11/35.**G.**
Str. 14/7—5/8/38.**L.**
Str. 16/2—27/3/41.**G.**
Str. 30/4—18/5/44.**G.**
Str. 5/4—25/5/46.**G.**

BOILERS:
540.
540 23/7/04.
119 24/3/22.
2337 10/12/24.
2321 1/2/30.
2379 4/7/32.
2377 15/11/35.
2368 27/3/41.
2356 18/5/44.

SHEDS:
Colchester.
Ipswich 20/8/37.
Cambridge 11/10/37.
Ipswich 7/1/38.
Stratford 13/12/40.
Colchester 19/1/46.

RENUMBERED:
7540 10/12/24.
5357 7/9/46.

CONDEMNED: 5/9/49.
Cut up at Stratford.

7541

Stratford.

To traffic 10/1888.

REPAIRS:
Str. ?/?—?/12/06.**G.**
Str. 27/3—11/8/20.**G.**
Str. 29/9/24—20/1/25.**G.**
Str. ?/?—?/7/29.**G.**
Str. 6—21/8/31.**G.**
Coal guard on tender.
Str. 12—23/3/34.**G.**

BOILERS:
541.
541 ?/12/06.
39 11/8/20.
535 20/1/25.
2376 ?/7/29.
2384 21/8/31.
2307 23/3/34.

SHEDS:
Colchester.
Ipswich 25/1/32.

RENUMBERED:
7541 20/1/25.

*SOLD: to London Film
Productions, Denham, 19/9/36.
Ex-Stratford 13/7/42 after
intermediate repair as WD221.
Cut up at Stratford in 1944.*

7830

Stratford.

To traffic 10/1888.

REPAIRS:
Str. ?/?—?/12/01.**G.**
Str. 25/1—30/4/21.**G.**
Records missing.
Str. ?/?—?/5/29.**G.**
Coal guard on tender.
Str. 18/7—9/8/32.**G.**
Str. 9—24/10/35.**G.**
Str. ?/?—16/9/38.**G.**
Str. ?/?—16/10/41.**G.**
Str. ?/?—9/3/44.**G.**
Str. ?/?—23/8/45.**G.**

BOILERS:
830.
830 ?/12/01.
597 30/4/21.
2353 ?/5/29.
2352 9/8/32.
2362 24/10/35.
2396 16/9/38.
2379 16/10/41.
2357 9/3/44.
2387 23/8/45.

SHEDS:
Norwich.
Yarmouth 9/10/28.
Norwich 27/7/30.
Lowestoft 1/12/40.
Norwich 4/7/43.

RENUMBERED:
7830 ?/?
5358 10/11/46.

CONDEMNED: 9/8/47.
Cut up at Stratford.

7831

Stratford.

To traffic 10/1888.

REPAIRS:
Str. ?/?—?/6/03.**G.**
Str. 17/5—1/11/18.**G.**

7831 cont./
Str. 3/5—21/10/21.**G.**
Str. 8/10—31/12/26.**G.**
Str. ?/?—?/6/29.**G.**
Coal guard on tender.
Str. 23/9—10/10/31.**G.**
Str. 6—20/7/34.**G.**

BOILERS:
831.
831 ?/6/03.
2340 1/11/18.
819 21/10/21.
2339 31/12/26.
2354 ?/6/29.
2369 10/10/31.
2393 20/7/34.

SHEDS:
Cambridge.
King's Lynn 27/10/29.
March 11/6/36.

RENUMBERED:
7831 *by* 25/2/25.

CONDEMNED: 30/11/36.

_____

(7)832

Stratford.

To traffic 10/1888.

REPAIRS:
Str. 10/2—14/8/03.**G.**
Str. 27/7—18/12/17.**G.**

BOILERS:
832.
832 14/8/03.
846 18/12/17.

SHED:
Cambridge.

CONDEMNED: 31/8/23.

_____

7833

Stratford.

To traffic 10/1888.

REPAIRS:
Str. ?/?—?/6/05.**G.**
Str. 7/9—23/12/21.**G.**
Str. 24/5—16/8/24.**G.**
Str. 12/1—12/3/27.**G.**
Coal guard on tender.
Str. 20/3—8/5/29.**G.**
Str. 15/10—24/11/31.**G.**
Str. 24/4—20/6/34.**G.**

Str. 11/4—10/6/37.**G.**
Frames altered.
Str. 15/6—24/7/41.**G.**
Str. 23/4—26/5/44.**G.**
Str. 20/10—22/11/46.**G.**
Str. 22—29/6/47.**L.**
Str. 1—21/1/50.**G.**
Str. 19/10—14/11/52.**G.**

BOILERS:
833.
833 ?/6/05.
838 23/12/21.
2320 12/3/27.
2343 8/5/29.
2350 24/11/31.
2394 20/6/34.
2726 10/6/37.
2791 24/7/41.
3349 26/5/44.
3385 22/11/46.
3340 21/1/50.
23568 14/11/52.

SHEDS:
Cambridge.
King's Lynn 19/10/34.
March 17/4/36.
King's Lynn 12/10/39.

RENUMBERED:
7833 16/8/24.
5359 20/10/46.
65359 21/1/50.

CONDEMNED: 5/12/55.
Cut up at Stratford.

_____

7834

Stratford.

To traffic 10/1888.

REPAIRS:
Str. 18/4—6/9/05.**G.**
Str. 29/3—29/6/17.**G.**
Str. 11/2—6/5/21.**G.**
Str. ?/?—?/9/24.**G.**
Str. 1/4—1/7/27.**G.**
Str. 19/10—2/11/29.**G.**
Coal guard on tender.
Str. 9—26/5/32.**G.**
Frames altered.
Str. 10/9—9/10/35.**G.**
Str. ?/?—12/9/38.**G.**
Str. ?/?—12/3/43.**G.**
Str. ?/?—21/6/45.**G.**

BOILERS:
834.
834 6/9/05.
869 29/6/17.
2313 6/5/21.

2358 1/7/27.
686 2/11/29.
2777 26/5/32.
2553 9/10/35.
3300 12/9/38.
3345 12/3/43.
3318 21/6/45.

SHEDS:
Cambridge.
King's Lynn 4/10/30.
Cambridge 1/11/31.
Norwich 14/4/33.
Lowestoft 7/4/34.
Norwich 9/6/34.
Lowestoft 29/9/34.
Norwich 10/11/34.

RENUMBERED:
7834 ?/9/24.
5360 20/10/46.

CONDEMNED: 4/11/47.
Cut up at Stratford.

_____

7835

Stratford.

To traffic 7/1889.

REPAIRS:
Str. ?/?—?/6/04.**G.**
Str. 14/11/19—24/3/20.**G.**
Str. 5/6—16/10/23.**G.**
Str. ?/?—?/7/26.**G.**
Str. ?/?—?/11/28.**G.**
Coal guard on tender.
Str. 24/8—5/9/31.**G.**
Str. 14—31/5/34.**G.**

BOILERS:
835.
835 ?/6/04.
40 24/3/20.
122 16/10/23.
2369 ?/11/28.
2394 5/9/31.
124 31/5/34.

SHEDS:
Cambridge.
King's Lynn 25/9/34.

RENUMBERED:
7835 ?/7/26.

SOLD: *to London Film
Productions, Denham,* 19/9/36.
*Became WD212. Cut up at
Stratford in 1944.*

_____

7836

Stratford.

To traffic 7/1889.

REPAIRS:
Str. ?/?—?/6/99.**G.**
Str. 15/4—19/8/14.**G.**
Str. 20/8—1/12/23.**G.**
Str. 21/5—18/9/26.**G.**
Coal guard on tender.
Str. 6/12/28—24/1/29.**G.**
Str. 6/8—18/9/31.**G.**
Str. 2—16/3/32.**L.**
Str. 3/4—5/5/34.**G.**
Str. 11/4—10/7/37.**G.**
Str. 26/6—23/8/41.**G.**
Str. 24/9—24/10/44.**G.**
Frames altered.
Str. 14/4—15/5/47.**G.**
Str. 4—8/4/48.**L.**
Str. 8—21/1/50.**G.**
Str. 5—23/1/53.**G.**
Str. 7/2—16/3/57.**G.**
Str. 24/11—17/12/60.**C/L.**

BOILERS:
836.
836 ?/6/99.
2303 19/8/14.
693 18/9/26.
2348 24/1/29.
613 18/9/31.
2373 5/5/34.
2379 10/7/37.
2344 23/8/41.
3359 24/10/44.
3355 15/5/47.
3318 21/1/50.
23573 23/1/53.
23550 16/3/57.

SHEDS:
Cambridge.
New England 10/8/38.
Doncaster 17/10/42.
Mexborough 24/10/42.
Melton Constable 19/4/43.
Stratford 1/5/43.
Colchester 22/10/50.
Ipswich 12/11/50.
Stratford 3/2/57.

RENUMBERED:
7836 18/9/26.
5361 11/1/47.
65361 21/1/50.

CONDEMNED: 16/9/62.
Cut up at Stratford.

_____

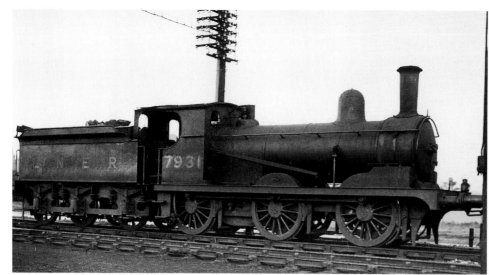

No.7931 also working from Peterborough East was similarly fitted by 1932. Peterborough East, 9th June 1935.

(left) The five Colne Valley engines, which got side window cab also, had a flexible connection between it and the back cab.

(below) For air raid precautions to prevent glare from the open door of the firebox, a tarpaulin sheet was fixed to the rear edge of the cab roof, and a light metal frame to support it was fitted on the tender. As it was a boon to the crew when running in reverse, it remained in position - and use - long after the need for its original purpose had gone.

Those with the side window cabs and vacuum ejectors at first had the ejector exhaust pipe through the boiler barrel (*see* page 31, bottom of 7941). From 1937, when later boilers were fitted, the exhaust pipe was placed outside the boiler.

The side window cab engines continued on the same jobs until withdrawal in 1958 and 1959; they also kept the heater connection at the front end.

Twelve dual-fitted J15's had London Passenger Transport Board trip cocks put on as a war time measure: 7641 (11th October 1940), 7644 (27th January 1940), 7646 (21st February 1941), 7552 (24th November 1939), 7554 (22nd January 1941), 7556 (20th April 1940), 7557 (31st October 1940), 7565 (24th August 1940), 7566 (26th March 1940), 7568 (20th February 1941), 7547 (4th December 1939), and 7548 (4th July 1940). At that stage, it was attached to the cab steps but when the need for it lapsed, it was removed. Between 22nd March and 15th April 1947, the same twelve, now renumbered 5441, 5444, 5446, 5450, 5452, 5454, 5455, 5463, 5464, 5466, 5475 and 5476, had the trip cock gear fitted on them again but in a modified position. They were for use on the Epping line. Stratford, 7th April 1957.

By 1947 the LPTB required that a trip cock be fitted within five feet of the leading end for both directions of running. On the right hand side it was now attached to the front guard iron, and on the left hand side (*see* previous illustration), to the tender frame between the middle and rear wheels. In addition, four more J15's were fitted with trip cock gear in February 1948: 5440 (17th), 5443 (6th), 5449 (6th), and 5453 (24th).

7837

Stratford.

To traffic 7/1889.

REPAIRS:
Str. 6/1—11/7/05.**G.**
Str. 1/10—14/12/20.**G.**
Cam. 19/4—29/6/23.**H.**
Str. 6/2—1/5/26.**G.**
Coal guard on tender.
Str. 3/4—14/7/28.**G.**
Str. 1/1—10/2/31.**G.**
Str. 13—28/12/32.**L.**
Str. 13/11—6/12/33.**G.**
Str. 7/6—10/8/36.**G.**
Str. 6/8—2/10/37.**G.**
Str. 18/3—24/5/40.**G.**
Str. 9/8—11/9/42.**H/I.**
Frames altered.
Str. 23/1—26/2/44.**G.**
Str. 27/10—2/12/46.**G.**
Str. 19/6/51. *Not repaired.*

BOILERS:
837.
837 11/7/05.
2357 14/12/20.
2311 1/5/26.
694 14/7/28.
2373 10/2/31.
2365 6/12/33.
2372 10/8/36.
2376 2/10/37.
2550 11/9/42.
2579 26/2/44.
3331 2/12/46.

SHEDS:
Cambridge.
Bury St Edmunds 10/12/39.
Cambridge 27/5/45.
Bury St Edmunds 19/5/46.

RENUMBERED:
7837 1/5/26.
5362 13/10/46.

CONDEMNED: 2/7/51.
Cut up at Stratford.

7838

Stratford.

To traffic 7/1889.

REPAIRS:
Str. 25/4—20/8/13.**G.**
Str. 16/6—14/10/21.**G.**
Str. 11/8—10/12/26.**G.**
Coal guard on tender.
Str. ?/?—?/3/29.**G.**
Str. 15/7—8/8/31.**G.**

BOILERS:
838.
838 20/8/13.
2300 14/10/21.
2366 10/12/26.
2342 ?/3/29.
2395 8/8/31.

SHEDS:
Cambridge.
King's Lynn 23/10/29.
Cambridge 29/12/29.

RENUMBERED:
838/7838 *at* 31/5/24.

CONDEMNED: 4/7/34.

7839

Stratford.

To traffic 7/1889.

REPAIRS:
Str. 17/8—25/10/10.**G.**
Str. 5/7—11/12/17.**G.**
Str. 18/3—7/9/21.**G.**
Str. 20/12/24—31/3/25.**G.**
Str. ?/?—?/10/27.**G.**
Coal guard on tender.
Str. 18/3—5/4/30.**G.**
Str. 18/7—10/8/32.**G.**
Frames altered.

BOILERS:
839.
839 25/10/10.
698 11/12/17.
38 7/9/21.
813 31/3/25.
685 5/4/30.
2510 10/8/32.

SHEDS:
Cambridge.
March 25/9/32.
Cambridge 20/10/33.

RENUMBERED:
7839 31/3/25.

CONDEMNED: 20/7/36.

7840

Stratford.

To traffic 7/1889.

REPAIRS:
Str. 5/6—6/11/13.**G.**
Cam. 19/10—7/12/22.**H.**
Str. 12/4—12/8/24.**G.**
Str. 30/4—10/9/26.**G.**
Str. 17/5—1/8/28.**G.**
Coal guard on tender.
Str. 13/1—20/2/31.**G.**
Str. 16/3—14/4/34.**G.**
Str. 15/11—22/12/36.**G.**
Str. 4/9—8/10/41.**G.**
Str. 26/3—6/5/44.**G.**
Frames altered.
Str. 1—30/9/46.**G.**

BOILERS:
840.
840 6/11/13.
595 12/8/24.
801 10/9/26.
124 1/8/28.
2316 20/2/31.
846 14/4/34.
2355 22/12/36.
2356 8/10/41.
2741 6/5/44.
3381 30/9/46.

SHEDS:
Cambridge.
March 24/1/37.
Norwich 24/3/37.
March 18/10/39.
Stratford 11/12/46.

RENUMBERED:
7840 12/8/24.
5363 27/9/46.

CONDEMNED: 1/8/49.
Cut up at Stratford.

7841

Stratford.

To traffic 7/1889.

REPAIRS:
Str. 20/8/13—9/1/14.**G.**
Records missing.
Str. *by* 17/1—?/3/25.**G.**
Str. ?/?—?/5/27.**G.**
Coal guard on tender.
Str. ?/?—?/8/29.**G.**
Str. 14—26/9/31.**G.**
Str. 26/3—14/4/34.**G.**

BOILERS:
841.
841 9/1/14.
699 ?/3/25.
2344 ?/8/29.
883 26/9/31.
2337 14/4/34.

SHEDS:
King's Lynn.
Cambridge ?/?/?.
Norwich 30/4/27.
Cambridge 7/10/27.
Norwich 24/12/27.
Ipswich 21/2/28.

RENUMBERED:
7841 ?/3/25.

CONDEMNED: 22/6/36.

7842

Stratford.

To traffic 7/1889.

REPAIRS:
Str. 15/6—17/11/99.**G.**
Str. 8/11/13—18/3/14.**G.**
Str. 28/1—27/4/21.**G.**
Str. 27/6—21/10/24.**G.**
Str. 9/4—18/6/27.**G.**
Str. ?/?—?/8/29.**G.**
Coal guard on tender.
Str. 13—24/6/32.**G.**

BOILERS:
842.
842 17/11/99.
2300 18/3/14.
689 27/4/21.
2374 18/6/27.
2315 ?/8/29.
2303 24/6/32.

SHEDS:
Cambridge.
King's Lynn 2/10/30.
Cambridge 9/3/33.
Ipswich 28/4/33.

RENUMBERED:
7842 21/10/24.

CONDEMNED: 13/11/34.

WORKS CODES:- Cam - Cambridge shed. Dar - Darlington. Don - Doncaster. Ips - Ipwich shed. Nor - Norwich shed. Pbo - Peterborough East shed. Str - Stratford.
REPAIR CODES:- **C/H** - Casual Heavy. **C/L** - Casual Light. **G** - General. **H** - Heavy. **H/I** - Heavy Intermediate. **L** - Light. **L/I** - Light Intermediate. **N/C** - Non-Classified.

7843

Stratford.

To traffic 7/1889.

REPAIRS:
Str. 23/3—25/8/05.**G**.
Str. 9/7—25/9/20.**G**.
Cam. 20/2—8/5/23.**H**.
Str. 17/10—3/12/25.**G**.
Str. 16/9—23/12/27.**G**.
Coal guard on tender.
Str. 19/3—25/4/30.**G**.
Str. 14/7—15/8/32.**G**.
Frames altered.
Str. 15/5—16/6/36.**G**.
Str. 15/10—30/11/40.**G**.
Str. 12—30/1/43.**L**.
Str. 5/12/43—20/1/44.**G**.
Str. 18/2—7/3/44.**L**.
Str. 29/9—9/10/44.**N/C**.
Str. 26/5—28/7/46.**G**.
Str. 15/6/49. *Not repaired.*

BOILERS:
843.
843 25/8/05.
2355 25/9/20.
2379 3/12/25.
2391 25/4/30.
2782 15/8/32.
2743 16/6/36.
2784 30/11/40.
2394 20/1/44.
2393 28/7/46.

SHEDS:
Cambridge.
March 25/9/32.
Cambridge 20/10/33.
New England 29/9/38.
Doncaster 17/10/42.
Barnsley 24/10/42.
March 22/12/42.
Cambridge 28/3/43.

RENUMBERED:
7843 3/12/25.
5364 17/11/46.

CONDEMNED: 20/6/49.
Cut up at Stratford.

7844

Stratford.

To traffic 7/1889.

REPAIRS:
Str. 3/9/03—13/2/04.**G**.
Str. 14/2—17/10/19.**G**.
Str. 25/3—10/7/24.**G**.

Str. ?/?—?/11/28.**G**.
Coal guard on tender.
Str. 7/1—19/2/31.**G**.
Str. 9—23/10/33.**G**.

BOILERS:
844.
844 13/2/04.
595 17/10/19.
538 10/7/24.
2365 19/2/31.
2317 23/10/33.

SHED:
Stratford.

RENUMBERED:
7844 10/7/24.

CONDEMNED: 1/8/36.

7845

Stratford.

To traffic 10/1889.

REPAIRS:
Str. ?/?—?/6/04.**G**.
Str. 4/6—11/9/20.**G**.
Str. 27/6—1/10/25.**G**.
Str. 25/11/27—1/2/28.**G**.
Coal guard on tender.
Str. 29/5—20/6/30.**G**.
Str. 26/9—14/10/32.**G**.
Str. 30/7—20/8/35.**G**.

BOILERS:
845.
845 ?/6/04.
852 11/9/20.
804 1/10/25.
2372 1/2/28.
813 20/6/30.
2389 14/10/32.
2341 20/8/35.

SHEDS:
Cambridge.
Norwich 18/9/36.
Lowestoft 24/1/37.
Norwich 14/2/37.

RENUMBERED:
7845 1/10/25.

CONDEMNED: 22/12/38.

7846

Stratford.

To traffic 10/1889.

REPAIRS:
Str. 28/8/13—5/2/14.**G**.
Str. 13/6—28/9/17.**G**.
Str. 1/7—17/9/20.**G**.
Cam. 15/5—31/7/22.**H**.
Str. 14/8—12/11/24.**G**.
Str. 21/4—24/6/27.**G**.
Coal guard on tender.
Str. 14/5—2/7/29.**G**.
Str. 21/7—27/8/31.**G**.
Str. 18/11—2/12/32.**L**.
Str. 9—31/8/34.**G**.
Str. 19/7—19/8/37.**G**.
Str. 23/9—26/10/40.**G**.
Str. 15/11—5/12/40.**L**.
Str. 4/3—28/4/44.**G**.
Str. 1—21/3/47.**G**.
Frames altered.
Str. 29/9—20/10/47.**L**.
Str. 3—5/12/48.**N/C**.

BOILERS:
846.
846 5/2/14.
539 28/9/17.
873 17/9/20.
849 24/6/27.
883 2/7/29.
2347 27/8/31.
2395 31/8/34.
2368 19/8/37.
2361 26/10/40.
2395 28/4/44.
3354 21/3/47.

SHEDS:
March.
Stratford 2/12/32.
Parkeston 20/3/43.

RENUMBERED:
7846 12/11/24.
5365 13/10/46.

CONDEMNED: 17/7/50.
Cut up at Stratford.

7847

Stratford.

To traffic 10/1889.

REPAIRS:
Str. 14/10/98—23/2/99.**G**.
Str. 8/6—12/8/15.**G**.
Str. 30/6/19—27/1/20.**G**.
Cam. 26/7—17/11/22.**H**.
Str. 6/9—6/12/24.**G**.
Str. 21/1—26/3/27.**G**.
Coal guard on tender.
Str. 17/1—5/3/29.**G**.
Str. 8/6—9/7/31.**G**.
Str. 21/3—5/5/34.**G**.

Parry soot blower fitted.
Str. 31/12/36—17/2/37.**G**.
Str. 16/6—12/7/40.**G**.
Str. 17/10—25/11/42.**G**.
Str. 6/5—1/6/45.**G**.
Str. 22/8—30/9/46.**G**.
Str. 9/3—2/4/49.**G**.
Str. 18/5/52. *Not repaired.*

BOILERS:
847.
847 23/2/99.
2316 12/8/15.
696 27/1/20.
613 26/3/27.
826 5/3/29.
124 9/7/31.
2360 5/5/34.
2357 17/2/37.
2363 12/7/40.
2374 25/11/42.
2363 1/6/45.
2384 30/9/46.
2391 2/4/49.

SHEDS:
King's Lynn.
March 2/7/34.
Cambridge 16/4/36.
Stratford 15/12/40.
Cambridge 23/4/41.
King's Lynn 26/10/41.
Cambridge 1/2/42.
March 26/4/49.

RENUMBERED:
7847 6/12/24.
5366 26/9/46.
65366 2/4/49.

CONDEMNED: 2/6/52.
Cut up at Stratford.

7848

Stratford.

To traffic 10/1889.

REPAIRS:
Str. 17/4—29/10/02.**G**.
Str. 29/9—20/2/17.**G**.
Cam. 27/9—30/11/23.**H**.
Str. 17/4—15/8/25.**G**.
Str. 9/3—22/6/28.**G**.
Coal guard on tender.
Str. 18/6—15/8/30.**G**.
Str. 7—25/11/32.**G**.
Str. 18/11—17/12/35.**G**.
Str. 26/1—4/4/40.**G**.
Str. 23/5—23/7/43.**G**.
Str. 30/4—17/5/45.**G**.
Str. 5/1—14/2/47.**G**.

7848 cont./
BOILERS:
 848.
 848 29/10/02.
2332 20/2/17.
 691 15/8/25.
2333 15/8/30.
2346 25/11/32.
2385 17/12/35.
2382 23/7/43.
2360 17/5/45.
2388 14/2/47.

SHEDS:
Cambridge.
Norwich 16/9/36.
Lowestoft 2/5/37.
Norwich 5/4/42.

RENUMBERED:
7848 15/8/25.
5367 21/10/46.

CONDEMNED: 2/1/50.
Cut up at Stratford.

_____

7849

Stratford.

To traffic 10/1889.

REPAIRS:
Str. 2/11/11—8/2/12.**G.**
Str. 11/11/16—8/3/17.**G.**
Str. 9—14/6/21.**N/C.**
Liquid fuel equipment fitted.
Str. 27/6—7/11/24.**G.**
Str. ?/?—?/8/27.**G.**
Coal guard on tender.
Str. 1—19/10/29.**G.**
Str. 14—29/3/32.**G.**
Str. 13—31/3/35.**G.**
Str. ?/?—16/7/38.**G.**
Str. ?/?—21/7/42.**G.**
Str. 19/5—7/6/45.**G.**

BOILERS:
 849.
 849 8/2/12.
2333 8/3/17.
2374 19/10/29.
2366 29/3/32.
2318 31/3/35.
2372 21/7/42.
2382 7/6/45.

SHEDS:
Cambridge.
Bury St Edmunds 10/12/39.
Cambridge ?/5/40.
South Lynn 29/1/43.
March 6/8/43.
King's Lynn 23/10/43.

RENUMBERED:
7849 7/11/24.
5368 20/10/46.

CONDEMNED: 29/5/48.
Cut up at Stratford.

_____

7850

Stratford.

To traffic 10/1889.

REPAIRS:
Str. 14/11/99—2/3/00.**G.**
Str. 22/4—4/9/14.**G.**
Str. 17/8—27/11/23.**G.**
Str. 12/6—16/9/25.**G.**
Str. 13/1—23/3/28.**G.**
Coal guard on tender.
Str. 5/4—9/5/30.**G.**
Str. 26/3—30/4/32.**G.**
Str. 18/7—16/8/35.**G.**
Str. 9/10—9/12/39.**G.**
Str. 7/3—26/4/41.**G.**
Str. 27/8—17/10/44.**G.**
Str. 4/11—22/12/47.**G.**

BOILERS:
 850.
 850 2/3/00.
2304 4/9/14.
 690 27/11/23.
 825 16/9/25.
 841 9/5/30.
2306 30/4/32.
2397 16/8/35.
2396 17/10/44.

SHEDS:
Stratford.
New England 13/9/35.
Doncaster 17/10/42.
Barnsley 24/10/42.
March 4/3/43.
Bury St Edmunds 19/9/43.
Cambridge 19/5/46.
Stratford 3/7/49.
Colchester 13/11/49.

RENUMBERED:
 850ᴇ 27/11/23.
7850 16/9/25.
5369 20/10/46.

CONDEMNED: 6/2/51.
Cut up at Stratford.

_____

7851

Stratford.

To traffic 10/1889.

REPAIRS:
Str. 11/5—27/7/11.**G.**
Str. 18/1—28/6/18.**G.**
Str. 29/8—28/11/24.**G.**
Coal guard fitted on tender
between these two works visits..
Str. 22/11—21/12/29.**G.**
Str. 9—22/2/32.**G.**
Str. 1—20/3/35.**G.**

BOILERS:
 851.
 851 27/7/11.
 832 28/6/18.
2321 28/11/24.
2324 21/12/29.
2318 22/2/32.
2355 20/3/35.

SHED:
Cambridge.

RENUMBERED:
7851 28/11/24.

CONDEMNED: 28/10/36.

_____

7852

Stratford.

To traffic 10/1889.

REPAIRS:
Str. ?/?—?/6/09.**G.**
Str. 26/4—30/6/20.**G.**
Str. 28/1—27/5/22.**G.**
Str. 28/7—6/11/24.**G.**
Str. 4/2—2/4/25.**L.**
Str. 19/8—20/11/26.**G.**
Coal guard on tender.
Diamond soot blower fitted.
Str. 5/5—12/7/28.**G.**
Soot blower removed.
Str. 14/6—30/7/30.**G.**
Str. 25/7—18/8/33.**G.**
Str. 13/7—24/8/36.**G.**
Str. 2/10—25/11/39.**G.**
Str. 30/1—9/4/43.**G.**
Str. 23/8—8/9/45.**G.**
Frames altered.
Str. 22/8—19/9/48.**G.**
Str. 6—16/11/49.**N/C.**
Str. 9/4—13/5/52.**G.**
Str. 3/4/56. Not repaired.

BOILERS:
 852.
 852 ?/6/09.
 618 30/6/20.
 854 20/11/26.
2309 12/7/28.
2331 30/7/30.
2387 18/8/33.

2365 24/8/36.
2392 25/11/39.
2362 9/4/43.
3372 8/9/45.
3370 19/9/48.
23550 13/5/52.

SHED:
Stratford.

RENUMBERED:
7852 6/11/24.
5370 12/1/47.
65370 18/9/48.

CONDEMNED: 23/4/56.
Cut up at Stratford.

_____

7853

Stratford.

To traffic 10/1889.

REPAIRS:
Str. ?/?—?/6/02.**G.**
Str. 21/12/15—18/4/16.**G.**
Str. 4/1—9/4/23.**G.**
Str. 24/6—6/9/24.**G.**
Str. 25/2—30/4/27.**G.**
Str. 1/6—10/7/29.**G.**
Coal guard on tender.
Str. 2/1—5/2/32.**G.**
Str. 28/4—12/6/35.**G.**
Frames altered.
Str. 25/9—7/10/36.**H.**
Str. 9/8—21/9/38.**G.**
Str. 22/2—11/3/42.**G.**
Str. 11—26/9/42.**L.**
Str. 17/9—14/10/44.**G.**
Str. 28/12/46—22/1/47.**G.**

BOILERS:
 853.
 853 ?/6/02.
2320 18/4/16.
 822 9/4/23.
 851 30/4/27.
2366 10/7/29.
2396 5/2/32.
2574 12/6/35.
2564 11/3/42.
3302 14/10/44.
3387 22/1/47.

SHEDS:
Stratford.
Cambridge 10/11/39.
Stratford 12/12/40.
Cambridge 23/4/41.
Bury St Edmunds 26/10/41.
Cambridge 23/11/41.

7853 cont./
RENUMBERED:
7853 6/9/24.
5371 17/11/46.

CONDEMNED: 12/12/49.
Cut up at Stratford.

_____

7854

Stratford.

To traffic 10/1889.

REPAIRS:
Str. ?/?—?/12/08.**G.**
Str. 24/4—24/6/20.**G.**
Pbo. 15/5—6/6/23.**H.**
Str. 16/3—9/7/25.**G.**
Str. 27/10/27—26/1/28.**G.**
Coal guard on tender.
Str. 20/12/29—1/2/30.**G.**
Str. 8/6—4/7/32.**G.**
Str. 11/8—22/9/36.**G.**
Str. 12/6—14/8/40.**G.**
Str. 11/2—8/3/42.**L.**
Str. 26/12/43—3/2/44.**G.**
Str. 25/10—3/11/44.**L.**
Str. 6/10—10/11/46.**G.**
Frames altered.
Str. 27/4—7/5/49.**C/L.**

BOILERS:
854.
854 ?/12/08.
825 24/6/20.
2334 9/7/25.
851 1/2/30.
2324 4/7/32.
2370 22/9/36.
2357 14/8/40.
2370 3/2/44.
3384 10/11/46.

SHEDS:
Peterborough East.
New England 8/6/37.
Doncaster 17/10/42.
March 18/10/42.
Cambridge 15/4/49.

RENUMBERED:
7854 9/7/25.
5372 2/11/46.
65372 7/5/49.

CONDEMNED: 19/9/49.
Cut up at Stratford.

_____

7855

Stratford.

To traffic 10/1889.

REPAIRS:
Str. 26/11/12—4/3/13.**G.**
Str. 30/11/17—12/4/18.**G.**
Str. 11—17/6/21.**N/C.**
Liquid fuel equipment fitted.
Str. ?/?—?/4/23.**G.**
Str. 12/12/23—25/3/24.**G.**
Str. 13/1—10/4/26.**G.**
Str. 23/6—4/9/28.**G.**
Coal guard on tender.
Str. 6/9—10/10/30.**G.**
Str. 1/4—6/5/32.**L.**
Str. 9/10—3/11/33.**G.**
Str. 29/11/36—15/1/37.**G.**
Str. 9/3—4/4/41.**G.**
Frames altered.
Str. 10/3—3/4/43.**L.**
Str. 27/12/43—11/2/44.**G.**
Str. 28/10—10/11/45.**G.**
Str. 25/4—19/6/47.**G.**

BOILERS:
855.
855 4/3/13.
538 12/4/18.
615 ?/4/23.
858 10/4/26.
2317 4/9/28.
2356 10/10/30.
2359 3/11/33.
846 15/1/37.
2579 4/4/41.
2784 11/2/44.
2778 10/11/45.
3332 19/6/47.

SHEDS:
Stratford.
Norwich 26/1/37.
Lowestoft 14/11/43.
Norwich 16/1/44.

RENUMBERED:
7855 25/3/24.
5373 10/11/46.

CONDEMNED: 23/10/50.
Cut up at Stratford.

_____

7856

Stratford.

To traffic 11/1889.

REPAIRS:
Str. 15/12/04—29/6/05.**G.**
Str. 22/9/16—8/3/17.**G.**
Str. 22/6—26/10/22.**G.**
Str. 2/7—12/11/26.**G.**
Str. ?/?—?/3/29.**G.**
Coal guard on tender.
Str. 30/6—17/7/31.**G.**
Str. 2—17/5/34.**G.**

BOILERS:
856.
856 29/6/05.
2331 8/3/17.
2327 26/10/22.
613 ?/3/29.
2357 17/7/31.
2316 17/5/34.

SHEDS:
Cambridge.
March 20/6/34.

RENUMBERED:
7856 by 31/5/24.

CONDEMNED: 20/10/36.

_____

7857

Stratford.

To traffic 11/1889.

REPAIRS:
Str. 23/7/02—7/1/03.**G.**
Str. 31/8—15/10/15.**G.**
Str. 14/8/22—10/1/23.**G.**
Str. 21/9—24/11/25.**G.**
Str. 1/2—1/5/28.**G.**
Coal guard on tender.
Str. 30/7—12/9/30.**G.**
Str. 11—31/7/33.**G.**
Str. 15/3—15/4/36.**G.**
Str. 13—16/6/39.**L.**
Str. 16/9—18/11/39.**G.**
Str. 7/2—13/3/43.**G.**
Frames altered.
Str. 27/3—19/4/45.**G.**
Str. 21/3—6/5/47.**G.**

BOILERS:
857.
857 7/1/03.
2318 15/10/15.
2309 10/1/23.
804 1/5/28.
2372 12/9/30.
2380 31/7/33.
2304 15/4/36.
2362 18/11/39.
2560 13/3/43.
3334 19/4/45.
3302 6/5/47.

SHEDS:
Cambridge.
March 23/2/35.
Stratford 15/4/36.
Colchester 10/5/47.
Lowestoft 11/4/48

RENUMBERED:
7857 24/11/25.

5374 9/1/47.

CONDEMNED: 20/11/50.
Cut up at Stratford.

_____

(7)858

Stratford.

To traffic 11/1889.

REPAIRS:
Str. 9/12/10—28/2/11.**G.**
Str. 7/12/17—6/6/18.**G.**
Str. 9—14/6/21.**N/C.**
Liquid fuel equipment fitted.

BOILERS:
858.
858 28/2/11.
2338 6/6/18.

SHED:
Peterborough East.

CONDEMNED: 13/3/23.

_____

7859

Stratford.

To traffic 11/1889.

REPAIRS:
Str. 9/7/04—13/1/05.**G.**
Str. 10/10/17—25/1/18.**G.**
Str. 4/2—29/6/22.**G.**
Str. ?/?—?/11/26.**G.**
Str. ?/?—?/3/29.**G.**
Coal guard on tender.
Str. 15/12/31—8/1/32.**G.**
Str. 17/9—4/10/35.**G.**

BOILERS:
859.
859 13/1/05.
839 25/1/18.
2339 29/6/22.
2301 ?/11/26.
634 ?/3/29.
2343 8/1/32.
2375 4/10/35.

SHEDS:
Peterborough East.
New England 30/4/39.
March 11/5/39.

RENUMBERED:
7859 by 11/9/24.

CONDEMNED: 2/6/39.

_____

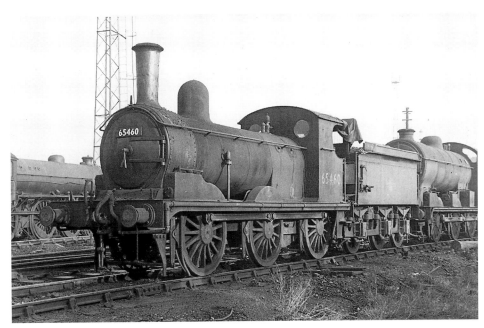

It was rare for this class to be used on Midland & Great Northern Railway lines but one or two did have the Whittaker tablet exchange apparatus fitted. The lower illustration on page 93 shows that No.7915 was fitted when at Yarmouth Beach in May 1944. Stratford, 1st January 1961.

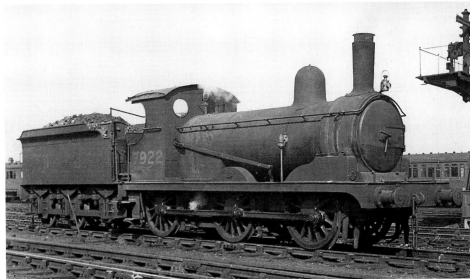

During 1940 three J15's, Nos.7837, 7922 and 7932, had a spark arrester fitted on a stovepipe chimney so that they could work at the ammunition dump at Barnham near Thetford. Cambridge, 8th July 1946.

On 7th March 1953, No.65420 (ex 7932) was ex works with the spark arrester restored but on a stovepipe chimney of medium length. Bury St Edmunds.

7860

Stratford.

To traffic 11/1889.

REPAIRS:
Str. 29/10/02—17/3/03.**G.**
Str. 24/11/14—3/3/15.**G.**
Str. 23/9—23/11/20.**G.**
Str. 15/6—15/9/22.**G.**
Str. 28/8—14/11/24.**G.**
Str. 15/12/26—12/2/27.**G.**
Str. 1/6—9/7/29.**G.**
Coal guard on tender.
Str. 9/1—6/2/32.**G.**
Str. 12/5—17/6/35.**G.**
Str. 19/6—8/8/38.**G.**
Frames altered.
Str. 26/7—6/9/41.**G.**
Str. 3—30/9/44.**G.**
Str. 17/1—10/3/47.**G.**

BOILERS:
 860.
 860 17/3/03.
2310 3/3/15.
2358 23/11/20.
2346 12/2/27.
2320 9/7/29.
2397 6/2/32.
2323 17/6/35.
2763 8/8/38.
2769 6/9/41.
2743 30/9/44.
2579 10/3/47.

SHEDS:
Stratford.
Southend 18/1/30.
Stratford 5/4/30.

RENUMBERED:
7860 14/11/24.
5375 23/6/46.

CONDEMNED: 21/11/49.
Cut up at Stratford.

_____

7861

Stratford.

To traffic 11/1889.

REPAIRS:
Str. ?/?—?/6/10.**G.**
Str. 9/5—23/12/19.**G.**
Str. 6/5—30/7/24.**G.**
Str. 25/3—23/7/26.**G.**
Str. 22/8—27/9/28.**G.**
Coal guard on tender.
Str. 10—21/11/30.**G.**
Str. 11—22/9/33.**G.**

BOILERS:
 861.
 861 ?/6/10.
2354 23/12/19.
 120 23/7/26.
 846 27/9/28.
2317 21/11/30.
2332 22/9/33.

SHED:
Stratford.

RENUMBERED:
7861 30/7/24.

CONDEMNED: 30/9/36.

_____

7862

Stratford.

To traffic 11/1889.

REPAIRS:
Str. ?/?—?/12/02.**G.**
Str. 14/1—15/4/21.**G.**
Str. 7—13/6/21.**N/C.**
Liquid fuel equipment fitted.
Records missing.
Str. 23/11/27—3/2/28.**G.**
Coal guard on tender.
Str. 11/6—11/7/30.**G.**
Str. 5—20/9/32.**G.**
Str. 16/9—1/10/35.**G.**

BOILERS:
 862.
 862 ?/12/02.
 829 15/4/21.
2360 3/2/28.
2304 11/7/30.
2377 20/9/32.
2389 1/10/35.

SHED:
Stratford.

RENUMBERED:
7862 ?/?

CONDEMNED: 16/11/38.

_____

7863

Stratford.

To traffic 11/1889.

REPAIRS:
Str. ?/?—?/12/01.**G.**
Str. 6/6—17/12/19.**G.**
Str. 23/3—10/12/21.**G.**
Records missing.

Str. 25/2—8/7/26.**G.**
Str. 28/7—19/10/28.**G.**
Coal guard on tender.
Str. 19—31/1/31.**G.**
Str. 2—19/10/33.**G.**

BOILERS:
 863.
 863 ?/12/01.
2342 17/12/19.
2361 8/7/26.
2383 19/10/28.
2307 31/1/31.
2382 19/10/33.

SHED:
Stratford.

RENUMBERED:
Still **863** *at* 17/1/25.
7863 8/7/26.

CONDEMNED: 24/10/36.

_____

7864

Stratford.

To traffic 11/1889.

REPAIRS:
Str. 21/9/03—31/3/04.**G.**
Str. 8/11/18—29/5/19.**G.**
Str. 27/8—20/11/23.**G.**
Str. 11/12/25—25/2/26.**G.**
Str. 4/2—3/5/28.**G.**
Coal guard on tender.
Str. 24/6—11/7/30.**G.**
Str. 15—31/8/32.**G.**
Str. 18/12/35—9/1/36.**G.**

BOILERS:
 864.
 864 31/3/04.
 805 29/5/19.
 40 20/11/23.
2317 25/2/26.
2351 3/5/28.
2302 11/7/30.
2378 31/8/32.
2352 9/1/36.

SHED:
Stratford.

RENUMBERED:
 864E 20/11/23.
7864 25/2/26.

CONDEMNED: 26/4/39.

_____

7865

Stratford.

To traffic 12/1889.

REPAIRS:
Str. 5/2—15/7/03.**G.**
Str. 19/4—15/7/18.**G.**
Str. 13/4—22/9/22.**G.**
Str. ?/?—12/12/22.**G.**
Str. 3/6—15/10/24.**G.**
Str. 3/9—1/12/26.**G.**
Str. 1/9—24/10/28.**G.**
Coal guard on tender.
Str. 25/4—6/6/31.**G.**
Str. 17/8—8/9/33.**G.**
Str. 16/3—16/5/35.**G.**
Str. 15/6—8/8/38.**G.**
Str. 8—29/11/41.**G.**
Frames altered.
Str. 2/2—3/4/44.**G.**
Str. 14/5—21/6/46.**G.**
Str. 17/6/49. *Not repaired.*

BOILERS:
 865.
 865 15/7/03.
 535 15/7/18.
 803 22/9/22.
2347 12/12/22.
2388 24/10/28.
2311 6/6/31.
2323 8/9/33.
2345 16/5/35.
2795 29/11/41.
2728 3/4/44.
2568 21/6/46.

SHEDS:
Stratford.
Parkeston 12/7/47.

RENUMBERED:
7865 15/10/24.
5376 7/6/46.

CONDEMNED: 27/6/49.
Cut up at Stratford.

_____

7866

Stratford.

To traffic 12/1889.

REPAIRS:
Str. ?/?—?/6/03.**G.**
Str. 10/10/19—23/1/20.**G.**
Str. 5/3—19/6/23.**G.**
Str. 18/6—30/10/25.**G.**
Str. 21/12/27—10/3/28.**G.**
Coal guard on tender.
Str. 26/6—8/8/30.**G.**

(above) **The normal GER type of snowplough was a large variety fitted to the end of the engine frame.**

In British Railway days at least sixteen J15's had their buffer beams drilled for attaching the small, Cowlairs type, of snowplough. Stratford.

(below) **The whole class depended on gravity sanding applied at each end of the coupled wheelbase.**

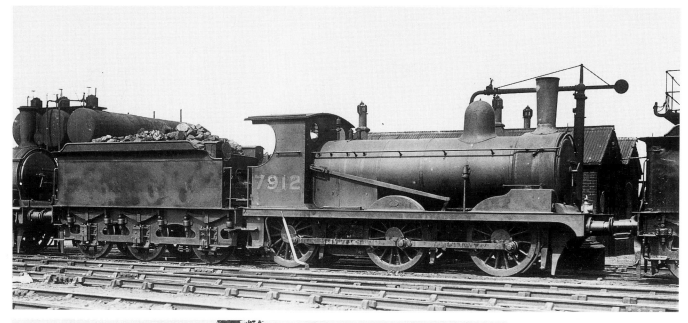

(above) Buffers with a parallel shank and hollow spindle were standard for the class and deviations were rare. None have been traced as having Group Standard buffers fitted.

(left) No.7561 in 1933, at Peterborough East, was an exception in having taper shank buffers with an end collar and solid spindle. No.7562 (see page 55, centre) was the only other one noted with taper shanks and as 65460 (see page 43, top) it had standard parallel shank buffers.

The Sharp Stewart built batch of J15's differed by having brake pull rods outside the wheels. Stratford shed, 15th June 1920.

7866 cont./
Str. 8/2—3/3/33.**G.**
Str. 2/2—13/3/35.**G.**
Str. 27/7—2/10/37.**G.**
Str. 25/8—17/9/41.**G.**
Str. 22/5—22/6/44.**G.**
Str. 21/3—24/5/47.**G.**

BOILERS:
866.
866 ?/6/03.
2343 23/1/20.
626 19/6/23.
809 30/10/25.
873 10/3/28.
810 8/8/30.
873 3/3/33.
2376 13/3/35.
2395 2/10/37.
2340 17/9/41.

SHEDS:
Norwich.
Ipswich 22/9/27.
New England 11/6/34.
Ipswich 24/11/34.

RENUMBERED:
7866 30/10/25.
5377 23/11/46.

CONDEMNED: 26/2/51.
Cut up at Stratford.

_____

7867

Stratford.

To traffic 12/1889.

REPAIRS:
Str. 13/5—29/11/04.**G.**
Str. 16/11—14/3/18.**G.**
Str. 8/1—31/3/24.**G.**
Str. ?/?—?/10/28.**G.**
Coal guard on tender.
Str. 29/1—19/2/31.**G.**
Str. 5—20/3/34.**G.**
Str. 13—18/12/35.**H.**
Boiler change only.

BOILERS:
867.
867 29/11/04.
2337 14/3/18.
807 31/3/24.
2360 19/2/31.
2388 20/3/34.
2379 18/12/35.

SHED:
Stratford.

RENUMBERED:
7867 31/3/24.

CONDEMNED: 25/5/37

_____

7868

Stratford.

To traffic 12/1889.

REPAIRS:
Str. 6/2—14/7/03.**G.**
Str. 19/10/17—15/2/18.**G.**
Str. 8/4—31/8/22.**G.**
Str. 12/8—4/11/24.**G.**
Str. ?/?—?/4/29.**G.**
Coal guard on tender.
Str. 8—24/9/31.**G.**

BOILERS:
868.
868 14/7/03.
2334 15/2/18.
887 31/8/22.
2350 ?/4/29.
2342 24/9/31.

SHED:
Stratford.

RENUMBERED:
7868 4/11/24.

CONDEMNED: 3/12/34.

_____

7869

Stratford.

To traffic 12/1889.

REPAIRS:
Str. 13/5—29/11/04.**G.**
Str. 25/1—17/4/17.**G.**
Str. 29/9/21—13/1/22.**G.**
Str. 18/10—15/12/23.**G.**
Str. 19/3—4/9/26.**G.**
Coal guard on tender.
Str. 10/8—2/11/28.**G.**
Str. 8/6—15/7/31.**G.**
Str. 17/4—18/5/34.**G.**
Str. 5/5—7/7/37.**G.**
Str. 22/10—10/11/38.**L.**
Str. 9/7—28/8/40.**G.**
Str. 9/9—12/10/40.**L.**
Str. 29/8—8/10/43.**G.**
Str. 4—21/9/45.**G.**
Frames altered.
Str. 25/7—28/8/48.**G.**

BOILERS:
869.

849 17/4/17.
801 13/1/22.
815 4/9/26.
2384 2/11/28.
2368 15/7/31.
2384 18/5/34.
2394 28/8/40.
2390 8/10/43.
3374 21/9/45.
3360 28/8/48.

SHEDS:
Stratford.
March 3/11/28.
Cambridge 31/12/28.
King's Lynn 27/1/29.
Cambridge 15/12/40.
King's Lynn 9/2/41.

RENUMBERED:
869E 15/12/23.
7869 4/9/26.
5378 11/1/47.
65378 28/8/48.

CONDEMNED: 23/4/51.
Cut up at Stratford.

_____

7870

Stratford.

To traffic 12/1889.

REPAIRS:
Str. 28/10/03—11/6/04.**G.**
Str. 22/11/18—8/4/19.**G.**
Str. 23/8—9/11/23.**G.**
Str. 30/6—21/9/27.**G.**
Coal guard on tender.
Str. ?/?—?/9/29.**G.**
Str. 23/11—5/12/31.**G.**

BOILERS:
870.
870 11/6/04.
2348 8/4/19.
2329 9/11/23.
689 21/9/27.
528 ?/9/29.
2327 5/12/31.

SHEDS:
Stratford.
Cambridge 21/10/27.

RENUMBERED:
Still **870** *at* 17/1/25.
7870 ?/?

CONDEMNED: 31/10/34.

_____

7871

Stratford.

To traffic 12/1889.

REPAIRS:
Str. ?/?—?/6/05.**G.**
Str. 18/8—10/10/22.**G.**
Str. 6/5—18/7/24.**G.**
Str. 31/3—28/8/26.**G.**
Str. 3/3—12/5/27.**G.**
Str. 7/11/29—25/1/30.**G.**
Coal guard on tender.
Str. 23/3—13/4/33.**G.**
Str. 15/5—23/6/36.**G.**
Str. 10/9—11/11/39.**G.**
Str. 24/10—18/11/43.**G.**
Str. 30/12/45—16/2/46.**G.**
Frames altered.
Str. 28/4—8/6/46.**L.**
Str. 15/6—31/7/47.**H.**

BOILERS:
871.
871 ?/6/05.
2305 10/10/22.
611 25/1/30.
2339 13/4/33.
2392 23/6/36.
2389 11/11/39.
2393 18/11/43.
3308 16/2/46.
3323 31/7/47.

SHEDS:
Stratford.
Norwich 28/8/26.
Yarmouth 9/10/28.
Norwich *at* 5/32.
New England 7/6/34.
Cambridge 15/11/34.
Stratford 12/12/40.
Cambridge 3/2/41.

RENUMBERED:
7871 18/7/24.
5379 24/11/46.

CONDEMNED: 8/9/49.
Cut up at Stratford.

_____

7872

Stratford.

To traffic 12/1889.

REPAIRS:
Str. ?/?—?/6/04.**G.**
Str. 10/10—31/12/23.**G.**
Records missing.
Str. 22/12/27—3/3/28.**G.**
Coal guard on tender.

Str. 4—27/3/30.**G.**
Str. 6—17/6/32.**G.**
Frames altered.
Str. 29/7—23/8/35.**G.**
Str. 9/6—2/7/36.**G.**
Str. ?/?—?/9/38.**G.**
Str. ?/?—22/12/42.**G.**
Str. 9—26/6/45.**G.**

BOILERS:
  872.
  872 ?/6/04.
2304 31/12/23.
  610 3/3/28.
  630 27/3/30.
2517 17/6/32.
2776 23/8/35.
2782 2/7/36.
2573 ?/9/38.
2548 22/12/42.
2567 26/6/45.

SHEDS:
Stratford.
Cambridge 10/11/39.
Stratford 15/12/40.
Parkeston ?/1/43.
Stratford 20/3/43.
Cambridge 2/5/47.

RENUMBERED:
7872 ?/?
5380 5/1/47.

CONDEMNED: 13/1/48.
Cut up at Stratford.

7873

Stratford.

To traffic 12/1889.

REPAIRS:
Str. 14/8—2/12/13.**G.**
Str. 13/3—11/5/20.**G.**
Str. 17/9—31/12/24.**G.**
Str. ?/8—?/10/27.**G.**
Coal guard on tender.
Str. 14—28/9/29.**G.**
Str. 16/12/31—2/1/32.**G.**

BOILERS:
  873.
  873 2/12/13.
  699 11/5/20.
  686 31/12/24.
2303 28/9/29.
2335 2/1/32.

SHEDS:
Stratford.
Ipswich 10/10/29.

RENUMBERED:
7873 31/12/24.

CONDEMNED: 19/12/34.

7874

Stratford.

To traffic 12/1889.

REPAIRS:
Str. 29/8—19/12/03.**G.**
Str. 25/1—19/4/18.**G.**
Str. 12/10/23—10/1/24.**G.**
Str. ?/7—?/8/28.**G.**
Coal guard on tender.
Str. 22/7—21/8/30.**G.**
Str. 8—28/9/32.**G.**
Str. 2—25/9/36.**G.**
Frames altered.
Str. ?/?—6/1/40.**G.**
Str. ?/?—23/6/43.**G.**
Str. 9/2—1/3/46.**G.**

BOILERS:
  874.
  874 19/12/03.
2336 19/4/18.
  891 10/1/24.
2365 ?/8/28.
2338 21/8/30.
2367 28/9/32.
2786 6/1/40.
2790 23/6/43.
2575 1/3/46.

SHEDS:
Stratford.
King's Lynn 8/11/33.
Stratford 8/2/34.
Parkeston 24/6/44.
Colchester 19/1/46.
Stratford 4/3/46.

RENUMBERED:
7874 ?/?
5381 22/12/46.

CONDEMNED: 25/11/48.
Cut up at Stratford.

7875

Stratford.

To traffic 8/1890.

REPAIRS:
Str. 22/12/03—16/7/04.**G.**
Str. 16/2—1/6/22.**G.**
Str. 20/6—15/8/24.**G.**
Str. 19/2—28/4/27.**G.**

Str. 20/9—12/10/29.**G.**
Coal guard on tender.
Str. 6/4—17/5/32.**G.**
Frames altered.
Str. 23/4—11/6/35.**G.**
Str. 12/7—31/8/38.**G.**
Str. 13/12/42—23/1/43.**G.**
Str. 4—21/3/45.**G.**
Str. 2/12/47—9/1/48.**G.**
Str. 2/3/52. *Not repaired.*

BOILERS:
  875.
  875 16/7/04.
2374 1/6/22.
  628 28/4/27.
2325 12/10/29.
2560 17/5/32.
2573 11/6/35.
2560 31/8/38.
3348 23/1/43.
2776 21/3/45.
3367 9/1/48.

SHEDS:
Stratford.
Cambridge 25/10/29.
King's Lynn 13/10/39.
Ipswich 7/1/50.

RENUMBERED:
7875 15/8/24.
5382 14/6/46.

CONDEMNED: 17/3/52.
Cut up at Stratford.

7876

Stratford.

To traffic 8/1890.

REPAIRS:
Str. 9/7—11/11/13.**G.**
Str. 17/8—8/12/21.**G.**
Str. 21/3—26/4/22.**G.**
Records missing.
Str. 1/3—23/5/28.**G.**
Coal guard on tender.
Str. 2—18/7/30.**G.**
Str. 24/11—9/12/32.**G.**
Str. ?/?—16/3/37.**G.**
Records missing.
Str. ?/?—19/2/43.**G.**
Str. 20/6—21/7/45.**G.**
Frames altered.

BOILERS:
  876.
  876 11/11/13.
  681 8/12/21.
2364 23/5/28.
2381 18/7/30.

2390 9/12/32.
2360 16/3/37.
2391 19/2/43.
2556 21/7/45.

SHEDS:
Stratford.
March 2/12/32.
Kings Lynn 11/12/33.
March 7/2/34.
Cambridge 20/6/34.
New England 20/7/39.
Cambridge 3/3/41.

RENUMBERED:
7876 *by* 25/2/25.
5383 11/8/46.

CONDEMNED: 6/2/48.
Cut up at Stratford.

7877

Stratford.

To traffic 8/1890.

REPAIRS:
Str. 14/3—17/7/13.**G.**
Str. 8/8/19—5/2/20.**G.**
Str. 9/2—26/4/24.**G.**
Str. 18/12/25—12/3/26.**G.**
Str. 28/4—24/8/28.**G.**
Coal guard on tender.
Str. 12/7—29/8/30.**G.**
Str. 12/12/32—6/1/33.**G.**
Str. 29/3—1/5/36.**G.**
Frames altered.
Str. 16/3—23/6/39.**G.**
Str. 4/2—15/3/40.**L.**
Str. 10/9—13/10/42.**G.**
Str. 8—26/7/45.**G.**
Str. 31/8—28/9/48.**G.**
Str. 20—26/11/49.**N/C.**
Fitted for snowplough.
Str. 14/3—26/4/52.**G.**

BOILERS:
  877.
  877 17/7/13.
  616 5/2/20.
  625 26/4/24.
2355 12/3/26.
2323 24/8/28.
2351 29/8/30.
2338 6/1/33.
3310 1/5/36.
2548 23/6/39.
3333 13/10/42.
3340 26/7/45.
3347 28/9/48.
23551 26/4/52.

All the Stratford built engines had the brake rigging between the inside faces of the wheels.

(above) The first two hundred and forty-nine built just had a steam brake on the engine with no provision for train braking, and all except seven remained so to withdrawal.

Of the last forty built, thirty-five were dual fitted for braking, having Westinghouse with a vacuum ejector for train brakes.

The other five, Nos.7645 to 7649, had Westinghouse brake only, both for engine and train until 1931/32.

These five had a vacuum ejector added for train brakes when ex works: 7645 (22nd September 1931), 7646 (22nd January 1932), 7647 (11th February 1932), 7648 (20th November 1931), and 7649 (26th February 1932). Near Brentwood, 15th July 1939.

7877 cont./
SHEDS:
Stratford.
Colchester 19/1/46.
Stratford 1/1/50.

RENUMBERED:
7877 26/4/24.
5384 12/1/47.
65384 25/9/48.

CONDEMNED: 28/3/55.
Cut up at Stratford.

___

7878

Stratford.

To traffic 8/1890.

REPAIRS:
Str. ?/?—?/12/01.**G.**
Str. 21/5—18/8/20.**G.**
Records missing.
Str. 21/5—15/10/26.**G.**
Str. 16/8—25/10/28.**G.**
Coal guard on tender.
Str. 8—24/10/30.**G.**
Str. 6—17/11/33.**G.**
Str. ?/?—3/2/37.**G.**
Records missing.
Str. ?/?—28/8/43.**G.**
Str. 17—29/11/45.**G.**

BOILERS:
878.
878 ?/12/01.
854 18/8/20.
2354 15/10/26.
2387 25/10/28.
2330 24/10/30.
2371 17/11/33.
2393 3/2/37.
2385 28/8/43.
2391 29/11/45.

SHEDS:
Stratford.
Colchester 19/1/46.
Stratford 16/5/48.

RENUMBERED:
Still **878** *at* 31/1/25.
7878 ?/?
5385 10/11/46.

CONDEMNED: 31/12/48.
Cut up at Stratford.

___

7879

Stratford.

To traffic 8/1890.

REPAIRS:
Str. 28/8/02—13/1/03.**G.**
Str. 9/5—29/8/17.**G.**
Str. 21/10—11/12/20.**G.**
Records missing.
Str. 23/12/26—12/2/27.**G.**

BOILERS:
879.
879 13/1/03.
690 29/8/17.
2360 11/12/20.
819 12/2/27.

SHED:
Stratford.

RENUMBERED:
7879 ?/?

CONDEMNED: 3/4/29.

___

7880

Stratford.

To traffic 9/1890.

REPAIRS:
Str. 7/11/99—22/3/00.**G.**
Str. 26/11/13—20/3/14.**G.**
Str. 9/5—18/12/19.**G.**
Str. 16/2—7/6/22.**G.**
Str. 25/8—21/11/24.**G.**
Str. 6/5—12/8/27.**G.**
Str. 20/9—19/10/29.**G.**
Coal guard on tender.
Str. 14/1—11/2/32.**G.**
Str. 12—31/7/34.**G.**
Str. 16/1—28/5/37.**G.**
Frames altered.
Str. 4/6—11/7/40.**G.**
Str. 5/12/43—1/1/44.**G.**
Str. 17/3—23/5/46.**G.**

BOILERS:
880.
880 22/3/00.
2301 20/3/14.
686 18/12/19.
2324 21/11/24.
2319 19/10/29.
2344 11/2/32.
2350 31/7/34.
2775 28/5/37.
2568 11/7/40.
2752 1/1/44.
2783 23/5/46.

SHEDS:
Stratford.
Ipswich 28/10/29.

RENUMBERED:
7880 21/11/24.
5386 22/12/46.

CONDEMNED: 9/1/50.
Cut up at Stratford.

___

7881

Stratford.

To traffic 9/1890.

REPAIRS:
Str. 22/6—15/10/03.**G.**
Str. 16/7—23/11/14.**G.**
Str. 21/5—27/8/20.**G.**
Str. 8/5—19/8/22.**G.**
Str. 13/11/24—17/2/25.**G.**
Str. 11/3—18/5/27.**G.**
Str. 18/5—5/7/29.**G.**
Coal guard on tender.
Str. 19/9—26/10/31.**G.**
Str. 3/3—12/4/35.**G.**
Frames altered.
Str. 24/4—27/5/38.**G.**
Str. 20/4—13/6/41.**G.**
Str. 20/8—4/11/44.**G.**
Str. 8/8—25/9/46.**G.**
Str. 29/7/49. *Not repaired.*

BOILERS:
881.
881 15/10/03.
2308 23/11/14.
121 27/8/20.
534 17/2/25.
2327 5/7/29.
2348 26/10/31.
2680 12/4/35.
2791 27/5/38.
2531 13/6/41.
3309 4/11/44.
2779 25/9/46.

SHED:
Stratford.

RENUMBERED:
7881 17/2/25.
5387 10/11/46.

CONDEMNED: 15/8/49.
Cut up at Stratford.

___

7883

Stratford.

To traffic 9/1890.

REPAIRS:
Str. 30/11/12—10/3/13.**G.**
Str. 26/6—15/10/21.**G.**
Str. 1/10—8/12/23.**G.**
Str. 23/10/25—3/2/26.**G.**
Str. 7/4—6/7/28.**G.**
Coal guard on tender.
Str. 12/7—28/8/30.**G.**
Str. 22/12/32—13/1/33.**G.**
Str. 13/1—14/2/36.**G.**
Str. 9/10—8/12/39.**G.**
Frames altered.
Str. 22/10—16/11/42.**H/I.**
Str. 2/7—4/8/44.**G.**
Str. 27/10—19/11/46.**G.**
Str. 22/8—20/9/47.**L.**
Str. 22/1—11/2/50.**G.**
Str. 11—13/11/51.**N/C.**
Str. 16/5—12/6/53.**G.**

BOILERS:
883.
883 10/3/13.
2317 15/10/21.
688 3/2/26.
873 28/8/30.
2358 13/1/33.
2346 14/2/36.
2528 8/12/39.
3358 4/8/44.
2763 19/11/46.
2793 11/2/50.
2793 reno.23535 13/11/51.
23578 12/6/53.

SHEDS:
Stratford.
Norwich 12/11/50.
Ipswich 16/3/52.
Norwich 14/9/52.
Ipswich 16/2/58.

RENUMBERED:
7883 3/2/26.
5388 23/6/46.
65388 11/2/50.

CONDEMNED: 22/5/59.
Cut up at Stratford.

___

WORKS CODES:- Cam - Cambridge shed. Dar - Darlington. Don - Doncaster. Ips - Ipwich shed. Nor - Norwich shed. Pbo - Peterborough East shed. Str - Stratford.
REPAIR CODES:- **C/H** - Casual Heavy. **C/L** - Casual Light. **G** - General. **H**- Heavy. **H/I** - Heavy Intermediate. **L** - Light. **L/I** - Light Intermediate. **N/C** - Non-Classified.

7886

Stratford.

To traffic 10/1890.

REPAIRS:
Str. 3/10/02—19/2/03.**G.**
Str. 6/7—13/11/17.**G.**
Dar. 12/6—29/10/23.**G.**
Str. 11/7—2/9/24.**L.**
Str. 23/12/26—24/2/27.**G.**
Str. 6/4—1/6/29.**G.**
Coal guard on tender.
Str. 15/2—12/3/32.**G.**
Str. 1/4—31/5/35.**G.**
Frames altered.
Str. 7/2—9/4/38.**G.**
Str. 23/6—2/8/41.**G.**
Str. 4/1—18/2/44.**G.**
Str. 2/12/45—2/1/46.**G.**
Str. 26/8—25/9/48.**G.**
Str. 13/10/48—23/2/49.**L.**
Str. 15/9—18/10/52.**G.**
Str. 17/3—26/4/57.**G.**

BOILERS:
886.
886 19/2/03.
818 13/11/17.
2377 29/10/23.
2355 1/6/29.
2341 12/3/32.
2559 31/5/35.
2764 2/8/41.
2742 18/2/44.
2781 2/1/46.
3314 25/9/48.
23566 18/10/52.
23583 26/4/57.

SHEDS:
Stratford.
Norwich 1/6/29.
Lowestoft 19/7/35.
Norwich 16/1/44.
Lowestoft 26/3/44.
Norwich 23/4/44.
Lowestoft 17/7/47.
Ipswich 2/12/56.
Parkeston 13/3/60.

RENUMBERED:
886ᴇ 29/10/23.
7886 2/9/24.
5389 25/8/46.
65389 25/9/48.

CONDEMNED: 12/4/60.
Cut up at Stratford.

7887

Stratford.

To traffic 10/1890.

REPAIRS:
Str. 3/10/12—3/1/13.**G.**
Str. 16/2—17/5/22.**G.**
Str. 6/5—12/7/24.**G.**
Str. 10/9—23/12/26.**G.**
Str. 30/3—23/5/29.**G.**
Coal guard on tender.
Str. 22/2—12/3/32.**G.**
Str. 11—19/5/33.**L.**
Vacuum brake and heating apparatus fitted.
Str. 7/8—14/9/34.**G.**
Str. 7—25/2/38.**G.**
Str. 13/4—14/5/41.**G.**
Str. 6—25/9/43.**L.**
Str. 28/5—14/7/44.**G.**
Str. 6/10—8/11/46.**G.**
Frames altered.
Str. 25/1—3/3/49.**G.**
Str. 21/10—3/11/49.**C/L.**
Str. 20/1—6/4/50.**C/L.**
Str. 9/3—5/4/52.**G.**
Str. 29/11—24/12/54.**G.**

BOILERS:
887.
887 3/1/13.
888 17/5/22.
803 23/5/29.
2362 12/3/32.
2369 14/9/34.
2344 25/2/38.
2386 14/5/41.
3353 8/11/46.
23547 5/4/52.
23511 24/12/54.

SHEDS:
Stratford.
Norwich 23/5/29.
Cambridge 26/8/33.
King's Lynn 23/9/33.
Cambridge 23/2/35.
Norwich 28/6/35.
Yarmouth 3/10/37.
Norwich 23/1/38.
Lowestoft 27/6/43.
Norwich 21/12/45.
Yarmouth 5/5/46.
Norwich 23/4/47.
Cambridge 20/5/51.
March 18/5/52.
Cambridge 10/8/52.
March 21/4/57.
King's Cross 16/6/57.
Neasden 23/6/57.

RENUMBERED:
7887 12/7/24.

5390 2/11/46.
65390 26/2/49

CONDEMNED: 13/12/58.
Cut up at Stratford.

7888

Stratford.

To traffic 10/1890.

REPAIRS:
Str. 21/8/13—6/2/14.**G.**
Str. 13—17/6/21.**N/C.**
Liquid fuel equipment fitted.
Str. 23/12/21—25/3/22.**G.**
Str. 6/7—15/9/23.**G.**
Str. 19/2—9/5/25.**G.**
Str. 14/1—1/4/27.**G.**
Str. 20/4—1/6/29.**G.**
Coal guard on tender.
Str. 6/5—7/6/32.**G.**
Vacuum brake added.
Str. 12—17/5/33.**L.**
Heating apparatus fitted.
Str. 17/7—17/8/34.**G.**
Cab altered and tender weatherboard fitted.
Str. 13—27/3/36.**G.**
Str. 12/4—7/5/38.**G.**
Str. 9/12/40—8/1/41.**G.**
Str. 27/2—8/4/43.**G.**
Frames altered.
Str. 18/11—8/12/45.**G.**
Str. 4/2—16/3/48.**G.**
Str. 17/2—18/3/50.**G.**
Str. 21/12/50—19/1/51.**C/L.**
Str. 7/9—4/10/52.**G.**
Str. 26/6—6/8/55.**G.**
Str. 18/6—18/8/56.**C/L.**

BOILERS:
888.
888 6/2/14.
630 25/3/22.
627 9/5/25.
2312 1/6/29.
2355 7/6/32.
2357 17/8/34.
2381 27/3/36.
2386 7/5/38.
2378 8/1/41.
3313 8/4/43.
2558 8/12/45.
3394 16/3/48.
3304 18/3/50.
3304 reno.23507 19/1/51.
23563 4/10/52.
23505 6/8/55.

SHEDS:
Stratford.
Norwich 1/6/29.

Yarmouth 10/7/32.
Cambridge 4/9/33.
King's Lynn 23/9/33.
Ipswich 17/8/34.
Colchester 24/9/34.
Stratford 10/3/40.
Colchester 17/3/40.
Cambridge 6/5/46.
Bury St Edmunds 10/8/52.
Cambridge 19/10/52.
Bury St Edmunds 11/10/53.

RENUMBERED:
7888 9/5/25.
5391 20/10/46.
ᴇ**5391** 16/3/48.
65391 18/3/50.

CONDEMNED: 1/12/58.
Cut up at Stratford.

7889

Stratford.

To traffic 10/1890.

REPAIRS:
Str. 16/12/02—17/4/03.**G.**
Str. 11/4—13/8/19.**G.**
Records missing.
Str. ?/?—?/10/25.**G.**
Str. ?/?—/3/28.**G.**
Coal guard on tender.
Str. 30/4—23/5/30.**G.**
Str. 28/6—18/7/32.**G.**

BOILERS:
889.
889 17/4/03.
2349 13/8/19.
2331 ?/10/25.
2378 23/5/30.
2329 18/7/32.

SHED:
Stratford.

RENUMBERED:
Still **889** *at* 31/5/24.
7889 10/25.

CONDEMNED: 17/10/35.

7890

Stratford.

To traffic 10/1890.

REPAIRS:
Str. 24/4—26/7/12.**G.**
Str. 18/5—5/11/21.**G.**

7890 cont./
Records missing.
Str. 18/3—6/5/27.**G.**
Coal guard on tender.
Str. ?/?—?/6/29.**G.**
Str. 29/10—13/11/31.**G.**

BOILERS:
890.
890 26/7/12.
838 6/5/27.
2300 ?/6/29.
2345 13/11/31.

SHEDS:
March.
Cambridge ?/?/?.
Stratford 6/5/27.

RENUMBERED:
7890 *by* 17/1/25.

CONDEMNED: 25/2/35.

___

7891

Stratford.

To traffic 11/1890.

REPAIRS:
Str. 13/5—16/8/12.**G.**
Str. 1/2—30/6/18.**G.**
Records missing.
Str. 8/1—8/4/25.**G.**
Str. ?/?—?/9/27.**G.**
Coal guard on tender.
Str. 7—26/10/29.**G.**
Str. 22/4—6/5/32.**G.**

BOILERS:
891.
891 16/8/12.
611 30/6/18.
2326 8/4/25.
699 26/10/29.
2374 6/5/32.

SHEDS:
Stratford.
Ipswich 1/11/29.

RENUMBERED:
7891 8/4/25.

CONDEMNED: 21/1/35.

___

7892

Stratford.

To traffic 11/1890.

REPAIRS:
Str. 14/7/99—28/3/00.**G.**
Str. 27/11/14—6/3/15.**G.**
Dar. 11/10/23—12/1/24.**G.**
Str. 14/8—25/10/28.**G.**
Coal guard on tender.
Str. 10—25/3/31.**G.**
Str. 4—16/6/34.**G.**
Str. ?/?—22/7/37.**G.**
Str. ?/?—9/10/40.**G.**
Str. ?/?—18/12/43.**G.**
Str. 6/2—17/4/46.**G.**

BOILERS:
892.
892 28/3/00.
894 6/3/15.
2348 12/1/24.
2357 25/10/28.
690 25/3/31.
2368 16/6/34.
2373 22/7/37.
2384 9/10/40.
2389 18/12/43.
2385 17/4/46.

SHEDS:
Stratford.
March 1/1/49.

RENUMBERED:
892E 12/1/24.
7892 ?/?
5392 17/4/46.

CONDEMNED: 13/5/49.
Cut up at Stratford.

___

7893

Stratford.

To traffic 11/1890.

REPAIRS:
Str. 25/11/03—7/7/04.**G.**
Str. 8/4—29/10/19.**G.**
Str. 18/10—2/12/21.**G.**
Str. 6/5—15/9/24.**G.**
Diamond soot blower fitted.
Str. 26/1—26/3/27.**G.**
Soot blower removed.
Str. 18/1—1/3/29.**G.**
Coal guard on tender.
Str. 5/9—5/10/31.**G.**
Str. 26/11/34—12/1/35.**G.**
Str. 27/2—26/4/38.**G.**
Str. 24/5—27/6/41.**G.**
Str. 6/8—1/9/44.**G.**
Str. 22—28/9/44.**L.**
Str. 15/3—5/4/46.**L.**
Str. 5/12/46—18/1/47.**G.**

BOILERS:
893.
893 7/7/04.
528 29/10/19.
2352 15/9/24.
883 26/3/27.
2314 1/3/29.
2376 5/10/31.
2383 12/1/35.
846 27/6/41.
2388 1/9/44.
2377 18/1/47.

SHEDS:
Stratford.
Norwich 24/6/44.
Stratford 27/6/44.
Cambridge 12/11/48.

RENUMBERED:
7893 15/9/24.
5393 23/6/46.

CONDEMNED: 3/8/49.
Cut up at Stratford.

___

7894

Stratford.

To traffic 11/1890.

REPAIRS:
Str. ?/?—?/6/03.**G.**
Str. 2/5—10/9/14.**G.**
Str. 15/5/19—?/?.**G.**
Str. 17/12/24—6/2/25.**G.**
Str. ?/?—?/10/28.**G.**
Coal guard on tender.
Str. 18/11—5/12/30.**G.**
Str. 19/9—12/10/33.**G.**
Str. ?/?—13/3/37.**G.**
Str. ?/?—21/6/40.**G.**
Str. ?/?—2/12/43.**G.**
Str. 1—19/12/45.**G.**

BOILERS:
894.
894 ?/6/03.
813 10/9/14.
2373 6/2/25.
2359 5/12/30.
2363 12/10/33.
2380 21/6/40.
2381 2/12/43.
2392 19/12/45.

SHEDS:
Stratford.
Norwich 27/6/44.

RENUMBERED:
7894 6/2/25.
5394 8/1/47.

CONDEMNED: 29/5/48.
Cut up at Stratford.

___

7895

Stratford.

To traffic 9/1891.

REPAIRS:
Str. ?/?—?/12/03.**G.**
Str. 9/12/13—28/4/14.**G.**
Str. 24/10/19—30/1/20.**G.**
Str. 17/6—10/10/24.**G.**
Str. 17/9/26—15/1/27.**G.**
Str. ?/?—?/2/29.**G.**
Coal guard on tender.
Str. 28/7—25/8/31.**G.**
Str. 28/11—15/12/33.**G.**
Str. ?/?—20/3/37.**G.**
Str. ?/?—27/4/40.**G.**
Str. ?/?—4/12/43.**G.**
Str. 5—19/1/46.**G.**
Str. 4—11/10/47.**L.**
Str. 6—9/12/47.**L.**

BOILERS:
895.
895 ?/12/03.
905 28/4/14.
2541 30/1/20.
2556 15/1/27.
2559 ?/2/29.
2654 25/8/31.
2572 15/12/33.
2779 27/4/40.
2768 4/12/43.
3322 19/1/46.

SHEDS:
Stratford.
March 1/1/49.

RENUMBERED:
7895 10/10/24.
5395 9/1/47.

CONDEMNED: 12/5/49.
Cut up at Stratford.

___

7896

Stratford.

To traffic 9/1891.

REPAIRS:
Str. ?/?—?/12/03.**G.**
Str. 28/7—17/11/14.**G.**
Str. 24/12/20—10/5/21.**G.**
Str. 25/5—7/10/25.**G.**
Str. 13/10/27—2/2/28.**G.**
Coal guard on tender.

Before getting their side window cabs, the Colne Valley line engines were made suitable for passenger train working. No.7941 got both vacuum ejector and steam heat on 5th May 1933; No.7911 got a vacuum ejector from 26th April 1932, and steam heat from 5th May 1933; No.7888 got the vacuum ejector on 7th June 1932, and steam heat from 17th May 1933. Nos.7523 (20th July 1934) and 7512 (11th January 1935) got vacuum ejectors and steam heating at the same repair as the cab alterations were carried out. Just two more changed from steam brake only: ex works 16th February 1933, No.7532 had a vacuum ejector added but never got steam heating fitted. Ex works 19th May 1933, No.7887 had both vacuum ejector and steam heat. These last two did not get side window cabs.

Steam brake only engines normally had 3-link loose couplings but a few were fitted with the screw type. Stratford, 17th July 1946.

Those not equipped with a Westinghouse pump also did not have a box cover on the cab front where the reversing rod emerged, although there was one exception - No.65391 (*see* page 37, bottom).

(*above*) Where a Westinghouse pump was fitted, it was standard to have a box cover on the cab front for the reversing rod.

(*right*) Until at least the 1930's the tender still carried a dial gauge to show the depth of water in the tank. No.7923 still had one to its withdrawal on 4th October 1934, as did No.7831 to 30th November 1936.

7896 cont./
Str. 22/5—13/6/30.**G.**
Str. 30/8—16/9/32.**G.**
Str. 22/8—18/9/35.**G.**

BOILERS:
896.
896 ?/12/03.
2505 17/11/14.
2525 7/10/25.
649 2/2/28.
2520 13/6/30.
2553 16/9/32.
2730 18/9/35.

SHEDS:
Stratford.
Cambridge 11/10/35.

RENUMBERED:
7896 7/10/25???

CONDEMNED: 16/3/39.

_____

7897

Stratford.

To traffic 9/1891.

REPAIRS:
Str. ?/?—?/12/07.**G.**
Str. 22/11/18—30/6/19.**G.**
Cam. 2/7—25/9/23.**H.**
Str. 26/10—15/1/26.**G.**
Str. 28/4—20/7/28.**G.**
Coal guard on tender.
Str. 21/1—20/2/31.**G.**
Str. 12/12/33—4/1/34.**G.**
Str. 15/11—30/12/36.**G.**
Str. 24/8—8/10/41.**G.**
Str. 6—26/8/44.**G.**
Str. 29/9—26/10/44.**H.**
Str. 14/5—4/7/47.**G.**

BOILERS:
897.
897 ?/12/07.
902 30/6/19.
512 15/1/26.
2525 20/2/31.
3309 4/1/34.
2562 30/12/36.
2559 8/10/41.
2528 26/8/44.
2572 26/10/44.
3334 4/7/47.

SHEDS:
Cambridge .
Norwich 25/3/37.
March 19/10/39.
King's Lynn 25/10/43.
Norwich 8/1/50.

Ipswich 15/1/50.

RENUMBERED:
7897 15/1/26.
5396 1/12/46.

CONDEMNED: 26/3/51.
Cut up at Stratford.

_____

7898

Stratford.

To traffic 9/1891.

REPAIRS:
Str. 10/11/04—30/3/05.**G.**
Str. 3/5—27/8/15.**G.**
Str. 12/11/20—25/1/21.**G.**
Str. 28/12/22—21/7/23.**G.**
Str. 12/6—1/10/25.**G.**
Str. 25/11/27—6/3/28.**G.**
Coal guard on tender.
Str. 21/2—25/3/30.**G.**
Str. 17/4—18/5/32.**G.**
Str. 22/7—4/9/35.**G.**
Str. 10/2—23/3/38.**G.**
Str. 3—27/5/41.**G.**
Str. 23/7—8/9/44.**G.**
Str. 17/11—12/12/46.**G.**
Str. 21/9/49. *Not repaired.*

BOILERS:
898.
898 30/3/05.
2510 27/8/15.
2549 25/1/21.
568 1/10/25.
2561 6/3/28.
2517 25/3/30.
2773 18/5/32.
2778 4/9/35.
2340 23/3/38.
2377 27/5/41.
2386 12/12/46.

SHEDS:
Stratford.
Colchester 5/12/42.
Stratford 29/1/44.

RENUMBERED:
7898 1/10/25
5397 14/11/46.

CONDEMNED: 26/9/49.
Cut up at Stratford.

_____

7899

Stratford.

To traffic 9/1891.

REPAIRS:
Str. 8/12/03—16/8/04.**G.**
Str. 22/11/18—4/3/19.**G.**
Records missing.
Str. 16/8—19/11/24.**G.**
Str. ?/?—?/12/26.**G.**
Str. ?/?—?/1/29.**G.**
Coal guard on tender.
Str. 10—26/6/31.**G.**
Str. 13—28/9/34.**G.**

BOILERS:
899.
899 16/8/04.
2533 4/3/19.
2743 ?/1/29.
2720 26/6/31.
2340 28/9/34.

SHED:
Stratford.

RENUMBERED:
7899 19/11/24.

CONDEMNED: 25/1/38.

_____

7900

Stratford.

To traffic 9/1891.

REPAIRS:
Str. ?/?—?/12/05.**G.**
Str. 27/9—20/12/18.**G.**
Str. 1/6—17/10/23.**G.**
Str. 18/8—31/10/27.**G.**
Str. ?/?—?/4/29.**G.**
Coal guard on tender.
Str. 25/1—6/2/32.**G.**

BOILERS:
900.
900 ?/12/05.
2534 20/12/18.
2507 17/10/23.
510 31/10/27.
2563 ?/4/29.
2541 6/2/32.

SHEDS:
Stratford.
Norwich 16/4/29.

RENUMBERED:
7900 ?/?

CONDEMNED: 19/12/34.

_____

7901

Stratford.

To traffic 10/1891.

REPAIRS:
Str. ?/?—?/6/03.**G.**
Str. 31/10—24/12/19.**G.**
Str. 8/8—27/10/22.**G.**
Str. 29/11/24—21/2/25.**G.**
Str. 1/4—24/6/27.**G.**
Str. 21/6—19/7/29.**G.**
Coal guard on tender.
Str. 26/9—30/11/31.**G.**
Str. 7/8—4/10/34.**G.**
Str. 31/10—19/11/37.**G.**
Str. 6/7—8/8/40.**G.**
Str. 27/11—11/12/43.**G.**
Str. 14—27/10/45.**G.**
Str. 22/1—27/4/48.**G.**
Str. 29/1/52. *Not repaired.*

BOILERS:
901.
901 ?/6/03.
2539 24/12/19.
2540 21/2/25.
2520 24/6/27.
2519 19/7/29.
2555 30/11/31.
2547 4/10/34.
2361 19/11/37.
2370 8/8/40.
2782 11/12/43.
3378 27/10/45.
2397 27/4/48.

SHEDS:
Stratford.
King's Lynn 10/8/29.
Stratford 5/9/29.
Norwich 24/6/44.

RENUMBERED:
7901 21/2/25.
5398 15/12/46.
65398 24/4/48.

CONDEMNED: 18/2/52.
Cut up at Stratford.

_____

7902

Stratford.

To traffic 10/1891.

REPAIRS:
Str. 12/7—30/11/06.**G.**
Str. 28/12/17—24/5/18.**G.**
Records missing.
Str. ?/?—?/3/25.**G.**
Str. ?/?—?/11/27.**G.**

7902 cont./
Coal guard on tender.
Str. 25/10—16/11/29.**G.**
Str. 3—19/2/32.**G.**
Str. 21/3—7/4/34.**G.**
Ongar accident damage.
Str. ?/?—18/6/38.**G.**
Str. ?/?—2/7/43.**G.**
Str. 6—13/10/45.**G.**

BOILERS:
 902.
 902 30/11/06.
2526 24/5/18.
2539 ?/3/25.
2551 16/11/29.
2520 19/2/32.
3313 7/4/34.
2720 18/6/38.
2773 ?/7/43.
3376 13/10/45.

SHEDS:
Stratford.
New England 13/6/34.
Boston 25/3/39.
New England 4/10/39.
Boston 11/11/39.
New England 4/1/40.
Cambridge 3/3/41.

RENUMBERED:
7902 ?/3/25.
5399 4/1/47.

CONDEMNED: 12/3/48
Cut up at Stratford.

___

7903

Stratford.

To traffic 10/1891.

REPAIRS:
Str. ?/?—?/6/03.**G.**
Str. 6/6—7/11/19.**G.**
Str. ?/?—?/2/22.**G.**
Records missing.
Str. ?/?—?/1/27.**G.**
Str. ?/?—?/4/29.**G.**
Coal guard on tender.
Str. 14/7—11/8/31.**G.**
Str. 19—30/11/34.**G.**

BOILERS:
 903.
 903 ?/6/03.
 507 7/11/19.
2510 ?/2/22.
2513 ?/1/27.
2515 ?/4/29.
2680 11/8/31.
2720 30/11/34.

SHED:
Stratford.

RENUMBERED:
7903 by 25/2/25.

CONDEMNED: 9/2/38.

___

7904

Stratford.

To traffic 10/1891.

REPAIRS:
Str. 30/9/05—19/1/06.**G.**
Str. 9/2—12/4/17.**G.**
Str. 23/3—16/10/19.**G.**
Str. 23/2—16/5/24.**G.**
Str. 9/9—3/12/27.**G.**
Coal guard on tender.
Str. 19/9—7/10/29.**G.**
Str. 27/7—23/8/32.**G.**
Str. 2—3/7/34.**L.**
Str. 16—27/7/35.**G.**
Str. ?/?—26/8/38.**G.**
Str. ?/?—12/6/43.**G.**
Str. 2—19/6/45.**G.**

BOILERS:
 904.
 904 19/1/06.
 911 12/4/17.
2514 16/5/24.
2502 3/12/27.
2544 7/10/29.
2730 23/8/32.
2560 27/7/35.
2773 26/8/38.
2788 12/6/43.
2744 19/6/45.

SHEDS:
Stratford.
Norwich 19/10/29.
Stratford 12/12/40.
Norwich 4/3/41.
Lowestoft 16/1/44.

RENUMBERED:
7904 16/5/24.
5400 18/11/46.

CONDEMNED: 18/2/48.
Cut up at Stratford.

___

7905

Stratford.

To traffic 10/1891.

REPAIRS:
Str. 15/12/02—3/7/03.**G.**
Str. 26/11/13—8/4/14.**G.**
Str. 24/10/19—6/2/20.**G.**
Str. ?/?—?/11/21.**G.**
Str. 19/11/25—24/2/26.**G.**
Str. 17/3—30/5/28.**G.**
Coal guard on tender.
Str. 7—25/7/30.**G.**
Str. 29/8—12/9/32.**G.**
Str. 4—22/11/35.**G.**

BOILERS:
 905.
 905 3/7/03.
2501 8/4/14.
2542 6/2/20.
 938 24/2/26.
 521 30/5/28.
2549 25/7/30.
2790 12/9/32.
2569 22/11/35.

SHED:
Stratford.

RENUMBERED:
7905 by 17/1/25.

CONDEMNED: 9/3/39.

___

7906

Stratford.

To traffic 10/1891.

REPAIRS:
Str. 5/5—3/10/05.**G.**
Str. 9/7—2/10/20.**G.**
Str. 24/5—16/10/23.**G.**
Str. 18/5—15/7/25.**G.**
Str. 9/12/27—13/3/28.**G.**
Coal guard on tender.
Str. 22/2—17/4/30.**G.**
Str. 25/6—22/7/32.**G.**
Str. 20/7—9/9/35.**G.**
Str. 27/11/39—5/1/40.**G.**
Str. 3/5—24/7/43.**G.**
Str. 22/4—12/5/45.**G.**
Str. 3/11—10/12/47.**G.**
Str. 16/8/51. *Not repaired.*

BOILERS:
 906.
 906 3/10/05.
 546 2/10/20.
 567 16/10/23.
2520 13/3/28.
2730 17/4/30.
2561 22/7/32.
2768 9/9/35.
2575 5/1/40.
2567 24/7/43.

3348 12/5/45.
2573 10/12/47.

SHEDS:
Stratford.
New England 14/10/35.
March 17/11/36.
King's Lynn 26/11/36.
Norwich 15/3/38.
Stratford 12/12/40.
Norwich 4/3/41.
Lowestoft 18/7/48.

RENUMBERED:
7906 15/7/25.
5401 25/8/46.

CONDEMNED: 3/9/51.
Cut up at Stratford.

___

7907

Stratford.

To traffic 10/1891.

REPAIRS:
Str. 9/9/03—2/3/04.**G.**
Str. 27/11/14—4/3/15.**G.**
Str. 23/8—16/12/18.**G.**
Str. 16/5—29/9/23.**G.**
Str. 24/4—15/8/25.**G.**
Str. 18/11/27—28/1/28.**G.**
Coal guard on tender.
Str. 1/3—17/4/30.**G.**
Str. 30/5—2/7/32.**G.**
Str. 29/7—11/9/35.**G.**
Str. 24/6—29/7/38.**G.**
Str. 20/6—1/8/42.**G.**
Str. 17/12/44—10/1/45.**G.**
Str. 2/9—23/10/47.**G.**

BOILERS:
 907.
 907 2/3/04.
 909 4/3/15.
2537 16/12/18.
2543 17/4/30.
2785 2/7/32.
2773 11/9/35.
3313 29/7/38.
3306 1/8/42.
2528 10/1/45.
3338 23/10/47.

SHEDS:
Stratford.
Cambridge 10/10/35.
Hitchin 29/2/36.
Cambridge 31/3/36.
March 16/4/36.
King's Lynn 28/9/36.
Cambridge 1/9/39.
Stratford 12/12/40.

7907 cont./
Cambridge 3/2/41.
Stratford 21/11/42.
Colchester 25/2/48.

RENUMBERED:
7907 15/8/25.
5402 28/7/46.

CONDEMNED: 23/10/50.
Cut up at Stratford.

_____

7908

Stratford.

To traffic 10/1891.

REPAIRS:
Str. 11/11/02—5/3/03.**G.**
Str. 23/4—30/9/14.**G.**
Str. 19/1—27/4/23.**G.**
Str. ?/?—?/2/25.**G.**
Str. 24/9—15/12/27.**G.**
Coal guard on tender.
Str. 24/7—29/8/30.**G.**
Str. 18/9—2/10/33.**G.**
Str. 16/1—3/2/36.**G.**
Str. ?/?—3/11/39.**G.**
Str. ?/?—28/5/43.**G.**
Str. 24/3—11/4/45.**G.**

BOILERS:
 908.
 908 5/3/03.
 2503 30/9/14.
 2554 27/4/23.
 2548 15/12/27.
 2578 29/8/30.
 2552 2/10/33.
 2790 3/2/36.
 2787 3/11/39.
 3300 28/5/43.
 3330 11/4/45.

SHEDS:
Cambridge .
March 25/10/31.
Norwich 18/9/36.
Stratford 12/12/40.
Norwich 3/2/41.

RENUMBERED:
7908 ?/2/25.
5403 17/11/46.

CONDEMNED: 9/8/47.
Cut up at Stratford.

_____

7909

Stratford.

To traffic 11/1891.

REPAIRS:
Str. 13/3—12/9/03.**G.**
Str. 29/7—16/11/14.**G.**
Str. 24/5—22/10/18.**G.**
Str. ?/?—?/12/24.**G.**
Str. ?/?—?/7/29.**G.**
Coal guard on tender.
Str. 13—31/10/31.**G.**

BOILERS:
 909.
 909 12/9/03.
 938 16/11/14.
 922 22/10/18.
 2555 ?/12/24.
 519 ?/7/29.
 2538 30/10/31.

SHEDS:
Stratford.
King's Lynn 4/5/27.
Stratford 10/8/29.

RENUMBERED:
7909 ?/12/24.

CONDEMNED: 15/1/35.

_____

7910

Stratford.

To traffic 11/1891.

REPAIRS:
Str. ?/?—?/12/05.**G.**
Str. 14/12/17—3/5/18.**G.**
Str. 14/9—10/11/21.**G.**
Str. 4/6—13/9/24.**G.**
Str. 25/3—27/8/26.**G.**
Coal guard on tender.
Str. 25/8—5/10/28.**G.**
Str. 22/12/30—30/1/31.**G.**
Str. 21/11—12/12/33.**G.**
Str. 16/10—28/11/36.**G.**
Str. 5/10—16/11/40.**G.**
Str. 25/12/43—28/1/44.**G.**
Str. 7/4—7/5/46.**G.**
Str. 18/9—21/10/48.**G.**
Str. 20/7—26/8/52.**G.**
Str. 12/10/56. *Not repaired.*

BOILERS:
 910.
 910 ?/12/05.
 2527 3/5/18.
 2535 13/9/24.
 2516 5/10/28.

2546 30/1/31.
2748 12/12/33.
2741 28/11/36.
2373 16/11/40.
2568 28/1/44.
2754 7/5/46.
3321 21/10/48.
23558 26/8/52.

SHEDS:
Stratford.
Norwich 7/5/47.
Ipswich 25/11/51.

RENUMBERED:
7910 13/9/24.
5404 19/11/46.
65404 16/10/48.

CONDEMNED: 29/10/56.
Cut up at Stratford.

_____

7911

Stratford.

To traffic 11/1891.

REPAIRS:
Str. ?/?—?/6/05.**G.**
Str. 4/8—18/12/16.**G.**
Str. 11/8—2/11/23.**G.**
Str. 21/1—19/3/27.**G.**
Str. 23/3—24/5/29.**G.**
Coal guard on tender.
Str. 8—28/9/29.**L.**
Str. 5—26/4/32.**G.**
Vacuum brake added.
Str. 19—30/9/32.**H.**
Str. 27/4—5/5/33.**L.**
Heating apparatus fitted.
Str. 17/7—27/9/34.**G.**
Cab altered.
Str. 2—30/10/36.**G.**
Str. 8—25/3/37.**L.**
Str. 20/10—16/11/38.**G.**
Str. 13/6—11/7/40.**G.**
Str. 10—26/2/42.**H/I.**
Str. 21/4—6/6/44.**G.**
Str. 24/5—30/6/46.**G.**
Str. 12/1—9/2/49.**G.**
Str. 2—27/10/51.**G.**
Str. 14/6—24/7/54.**G.**

BOILERS:
 911.
 911 ?/6/05.
 2520 18/12/16.
 2510 19/3/27.
 510 24/5/29.
 2528 26/4/32.
 3323 27/9/34.
 2769 16/11/38.
 2778 11/7/40.

3323 26/2/42.
2763 6/6/44.
3305 30/6/46.
3333 9/2/49.
23531 27/10/51.
23514 24/7/54.

SHEDS:
Stratford.
Norwich 24/5/29.
Yarmouth 19/6/32.
Norwich 5/8/33.
Cambridge 25/8/33.
King's Lynn 23/9/33.
Cambridge 25/9/34.
Bury St Edmunds 10/8/52.
Cambridge 19/10/52.
Bury St Edmunds 11/10/53.
King's Cross 16/6/57.
Neasden 23/6/57.

RENUMBERED:
 7911 *after* 17/1/25.
 5405 8/12/46.
65405 5/2/49.

CONDEMNED: 16/8/58.
Cut up at Stratford.

_____

7912

Stratford.

To traffic 11/1891.

REPAIRS:
Str. ?/?—12/03.**G.**
Str. 1/3—1/7/18.**G.**
Records missing.
Str. ?/?—?/1/25.**G.**
Str. ?/?—?/6/27.**G.**
Coal guard on tender.
Str. ?/?—?/7/29.**G.**
Str. 1—15/1/32.**G.**
Str. 22/5—7/6/35.**G.**

BOILERS:
 912.
 912 ?/12/03.
 2530 1/7/18.
 2508 ?/1/25.
 546 ?/7/29.
 2767 15/1/32.
 2564 7/6/35.

SHED:
Stratford.

RENUMBERED:
7912 ?/1/25.

CONDEMNED: 31/10/38.

_____

During the middle 1930's it became customary to remove these dial gauges from the tender.

During and after the second war it also became usual to take off the left hand toolbox.

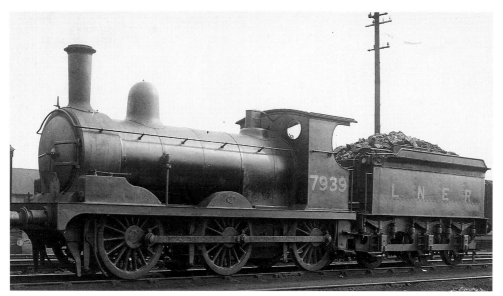

The standard tender held 2640 gallons of water and those built to August 1892 had semi-elliptical slots in the frames.

(above) From No.941 onwards, built August 1892, the frame slots were changed to be level at the top and bottom with semi-circular ends to them.

The first ten J15's built for passenger work in 1899, Nos. 640 to 649, were fitted with the 3066 gallon Worsdell tender, taken from GER G14 class 2-4-0 engines.

7913

Stratford.

To traffic 11/1891.

REPAIRS:
Str. 26/5—2/12/02.**G.**
Str. 30/4—9/7/18.**G.**
Str. 9/8—7/10/22.**G.**
Str. 16/9—21/11/24.**G.**
Str. 1/4—1/7/27.**G.**
Str. 29/6—17/8/29.**G.**
Coal guard on tender.
Str. 2—30/3/32.**G.**
Str. 3/5—22/6/34.**G.**
Str. 9/6—17/7/37.**G.**
Str. 22/6—2/8/40.**G.**
Str. 6—25/9/42.**G.**
Str. 18/6—26/7/44.**G.**
Str. 28/9—28/11/47.**G.**

BOILERS:
913.
913 2/12/02.
2532 9/7/18.
921 21/11/24.
513 17/8/29.
2551 30/3/32.
2746 22/6/34.
2394 17/7/37.
2775 2/8/40.
3332 25/9/42.
3357 26/7/44.

SHEDS:
Stratford.
King's Lynn 5/9/29.
Bury St Edmunds 24/9/40.
Cambridge 17/2/46.

RENUMBERED:
7913 21/11/24.
5406 8/12/46.

CONDEMNED: 2/4/51.
Cut up at Stratford.

7914

Stratford.

To traffic 11/1891.

REPAIRS:
Str. ?/?—?/6/03.**G.**
Str. 14/10/14—6/1/15.**G.**
Str. 22/8—29/10/20.**G.**
Str. 17/5—26/9/24.**G.**
Str. 29/10/26—4/2/27.**G.**
Str. 25/1—25/3/29.**G.**
Coal guard on tender.
Str. 8/5—30/6/31.**G.**
Str. 21/9—17/10/33.**G.**

Str. 21/5—27/6/35.**G.**
Str. 11/5—7/6/38.**G.**
Str. 19/2—20/3/43.**G.**
Str. 17/6—14/7/45.**G.**
Str. 18/2—6/5/48.**G.**

BOILERS:
914.
914 ?/6/03.
2506 6/1/15.
549 29/10/20.
2563 4/2/27.
2533 25/3/29.
551 30/6/31.
2548 17/10/33.
2767 27/6/35.
2750 7/6/38.
3346 20/3/43.
3369 14/7/45.
3397 6/5/48.

SHED:
Ipswich.

RENUMBERED:
7914 26/9/24.
5407 1/12/46.
65407 1/5/48.

CONDEMNED: 5/4/51.
Cut up at Stratford.

7915

Stratford.

To traffic 11/1891.

REPAIRS:
Str. ?/?—?/12/04.**G.**
Str. 28/2—2/7/19.**G.**
Str. 28/5—14/7/21.**G.**
Str. 24/3—5/6/24.**G.**
Str. 25/2—14/7/26.**G.**
Str. 17/8—9/11/28.**G.**
Coal guard on tender.
Str. 25/4—23/6/31.**G.**
Str. 19/8—28/9/34.**G.**
Str. 22/11—11/12/37.**G.**
Str. 7/3—15/5/43.**G.**
Str. 15/5—7/6/45.**G.**
Str. 27/10/47—6/1/48.**G.**
Str. 26/10—27/12/48.**H.**
Str. 14—27/1/50.**C/H.**
Str. 24/11/51. *Not repaired.*

BOILERS:
915.
915 ?/12/04.
519 2/7/19.
2515 5/6/24.
2500 9/11/28.
2523 23/6/31.
2344 28/9/34.

2547 11/12/37.
2556 15/5/43.
3300 7/6/45.
3384 27/1/50.

SHEDS:
Stratford.
Norwich 30/5/39.
Lowestoft 29/10/39.
Norwich 4/7/43.
Yarmouth Beach 30/4/44.
Norwich 4/6/44.
Ipswich 24/8/49.

RENUMBERED:
7915 5/6/24.
5408 7/1/47.
65408 24/12/48.

CONDEMNED: 10/12/51.
Cut up at Stratford.

7916

Stratford.

To traffic 11/1891.

REPAIRS:
Str. 21/10/03—20/4/04.**G.**
Str. ?/?—?/2/22.**G.**
Str. 6/12/23—11/3/24.**G.**
Str. 29/3—9/7/26.**G.**
Str. 30/6—5/9/28.**G.**
Coal guard on tender.
Str. 24/9—17/10/30.**G.**
Str. 19/1—2/2/34.**G.**

BOILERS:
916.
916 20/4/04.
2513 ?/2/22.
2538 11/3/24.
525 9/7/26.
938 5/9/28.
2522 17/10/30.
2525 2/2/34.

SHED:
Stratford.

RENUMBERED:
7916 11/3/24.

CONDEMNED: 9/4/37.

7917

Stratford.

To traffic 11/1891.

REPAIRS:
Str. ?/?—?/12/04.**G.**
Str. 24/12/20—18/3/21.**G.**
Str. 2/12/25—11/3/26.**G.**
Str. ?/6—?/7/28.**G.**
Coal guard on tender.
Str. 7—30/7/30.**G.**
Str. 30/8—16/9/32.**G.**
Str. 21/10—4/11/35.**G.**

BOILERS:
917.
917 ?/12/04.
2550 18/3/21.
2522 11/3/26.
2575 30/7/30.
2792 16/9/32.
2539 4/11/35.

SHED:
Stratford.

RENUMBERED:
Still **917** *at* 17/1/25.
7917 11/3/26 ???

CONDEMNED: 9/3/39.

7918

Stratford.

To traffic 11/1891.

REPAIRS:
Str. ?/?—?/6/06.**G.**
Str. 18/9/23—14/2/24.**G.**
Str. 11/12/25—20/2/26.**G.**
Str. 31/3—6/7/28.**G.**
Coal guard on tender.
Str. 13/9—17/10/30.**G.**
Str. 9—26/5/33.**G.**
Str. 14/2—19/3/36.**G.**
Str. 5/7—16/8/38.**G.**
Str. 24/9—11/10/41.**G.**
Str. 12/3—19/4/44.**G.**
Str. 11/8—4/9/46.**G.**
Str. 1/11/49. *Not repaired.*

BOILERS:
918.
918 ?/6/06.
2506 14/2/24.
2546 6/7/28.
2565 17/10/30.
2568 26/5/33.
2388 19/3/36.
2395 11/10/41.
2384 19/4/44.
2394 4/9/46.

SHEDS:
Stratford.
Peterborough East 31/1/31.

7918 cont./
Parkeston 30/6/31.
Ipswich 19/6/33.

RENUMBERED:
Still **918** *at* 14/2/24.
7918 20/2/26.
5409 30/8/46.

CONDEMNED: 14/11/49.
Cut up at Stratford.

_____

7919

Stratford.

To traffic 12/1891.

REPAIRS:
Str. 17/3—10/7/06.**G.**
Str. 16/11/17—9/4/18.**G.**
Str. 18/4—14/8/23.**G.**
Str. 17/8—4/11/25.**G.**
Str. ?/?—?/6/29.**G.**
Coal guard on tender.
Str. 11—27/7/32.**G.**

BOILERS:
919.
919 10/7/06.
937 9/4/18.
919 14/8/23.
519 4/11/25.
2557 ?/6/29.
2511 27/7/32.

SHEDS:
Peterborough East.
New England 26/3/36.

RENUMBERED:
7919 4/11/25.

CONDEMNED: 22/6/36.

_____

7920

Stratford.

To traffic 12/1891.

REPAIRS:
Str. 30/9/03—20/2/04.**G.**
Str. 15/9/16—8/3/17.**G.**
Str. 5/2—25/5/23.**G.**
Str. 15/3—7/6/28.**G.**
Coal guard on tender.
Str. 18/6—11/7/30.**G.**
Str. 1—16/6/33.**G.**
Str. 29/4—14/5/36.**G.**
Str. ?/?—10/1/39.**G.**
Str. 26/2—8/4/40.**G.**
Str. ?/?—2/7/43.**G.**

Str. 10—24/11/45.**G.**
Str. 26/1/48. *Not repaired.*

BOILERS:
920.
920 20/2/04.
2524 8/3/17.
2523 25/5/23.
542 7/6/28.
2534 11/7/30.
3303 16/6/33.
2565 14/5/36.
2571 8/4/40.
3308 2/7/43.
3341 24/11/45.

SHEDS:
Cambridge .
Stratford 26/6/26.
Cambridge 1/5/47.

RENUMBERED:
Still **920** *at* 28/4/25.
7920 ?/?
5410 26/7/46.

CONDEMNED: 6/2/48.
Cut up at Stratford.

_____

7921

Stratford.

To traffic 12/1891.

REPAIRS:
Str. 6/7—15/9/11.**G.**
Str. 1/9/16—8/3/17.**G.**
Str. 11/11/21—3/2/22.**G.**
Str. 24/4—14/8/26.**G.**
Str. 10/8—17/10/28.**G.**
Coal guard on tender.
Str. 18/3—8/4/31.**G.**
Parry soot blower fitted.
Str. 13—28/2/34.**G.**
Soot blower removed.
Str. 17—28/8/36.**G.**
Str. ?/?—2/3/40.**G.**
Str. ?/?—6/8/43.**G.**
Str. 9—23/6/45.**G.**
Str. 20/3/48. *Not repaired.*

BOILERS:
921.
921 15/9/11.
2525 8/3/17.
933 3/2/22.
2542 14/8/26.
2571 17/10/28.
2504 8/4/31.
526 28/2/34.
2571 28/8/36.
2747 2/3/40.
2557 6/8/43.

3370 23/6/45.

SHEDS:
Cambridge .
King's Lynn 24/10/29.
Cambridge 29/12/29.
March 25/10/31.
King's Lynn 28/9/36.
March 24/1/37.
Norwich 25/3/37.

RENUMBERED:
7921 ?/?
5411 8/12/46.

CONDEMNED: 15/4/48.
Cut up at Stratford.

_____

7922

Stratford.

To traffic 12/1891.

REPAIRS:
Str. 8/11/12—6/2/13.**G.**
Str. 14/12/17—4/6/18.**G.**
Str. 21/11/22—4/4/23.**G.**
Str. 9/2—13/5/25.**G.**
Str. 29/4—8/7/27.**G.**
Coal guard on tender.
Str. 14/5—5/7/29.**G.**
Str. 29/5—17/7/31.**G.**
Str. 18/4—9/6/34.**G.**
Str. 21/9—15/10/35.**H.**
Str. 8/12/36—11/3/37.**G.**
Str. 18/6—15/7/40.**G.**
Str. 10—13/12/40.**L.**
Str. 21/11/43—8/1/44.**G.**
Str. 2—17/5/46.**L.**
Str. 27/7—1/9/46.**G.**
Str. 28/6—5/8/48.**G.**
Str. 16/10/49. *Not repaired.*

BOILERS:
922.
922 6/2/13.
2528 4/6/18.
513 13/5/25.
2513 5/7/29.
2746 17/7/31.
2536 9/6/34.
2727 11/3/37.
2742 15/7/40.
2779 8/1/44.
2576 1/9/46.
3318 5/8/48.

SHEDS:
Stratford.
March 29/11/27.
Stratford 19/6/28.
March 13/10/28.
Cambridge 9/6/36.

Stratford 13/12/40.
Cambridge 11/11/41.
Stratford 12/11/48.

RENUMBERED:
7922 13/5/25.
5412 15/12/46.
65412 5/8/48.

CONDEMNED: 24/10/49.
Cut up at Stratford.

_____

7923

Stratford.

To traffic 12/1891.

REPAIRS:
Str. ?/?—?/12/01.**G.**
Str. 17/8—11/10/15.**G.**
Str. 7/5—20/8/20.**G.**
Str. *In by* 17/1/25—?/3/25.**G.**
Str. ?/?—?/8/27.**G.**
Coal guard on tender.
Str. ?/?—?/9/29.**G.**
Str. 2—14/11/31.**G.**

BOILERS:
923.
923 ?/12/01.
2514 11/10/15.
2545 20/8/20.
2551 ?/3/25.
2508 ?/9/29.
922 14/11/31.

SHEDS:
Stratford.
March 30/11/27.
Stratford 19/6/28.
March 13/10/28.

RENUMBERED:
7923 ?/3/25.

CONDEMNED: 4/10/34.

_____

7924

Stratford.

To traffic 12/1891.

REPAIRS:
Str. 4/10/01—17/3/02.**G.**
Str. 10/7—29/10/14.**G.**
Pbo. 27/9—6/11/22.**H.**
Str. 18/2—17/6/25.**G.**
Str. 22/12/27—15/3/28.**G.**
Coal guard on tender.
Str. 12/7—5/9/30.**G.**
Str. 14/3—6/4/33.**G.**

These large capacity tenders had 6ins. deeper sides than the 2640 gallons type.

(below) The last thirty built, Nos.7542 to 7571 were first fitted with 2640 gallons tender, but all of them were second hand. Nos. 552 to 561 got Holden tenders from withdrawn 2-2-2's, whilst Nos.562 to 571 got their tenders from GER Class P43 4-2-2, Nos.10 to 19. Nos.542 to 551 got spares from Holden 2-4-0's.

Changing of tenders led to some of Bromley types running with J15 class engines. They could be identified by the equally spaced axles.

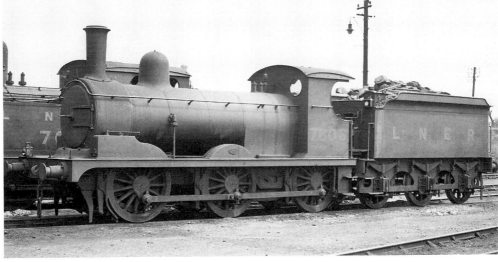

By the end of the LNER the 2640 gallons tender with unequal spacing of axles was standard for the one hundred and twenty-seven survivors. Colchester shed.

In April and June 1951, Nos.65447 and 65451 had, in turn, spare water cart tender No.8892 coupled. This held 2790 gallons but was only a temporary coupling. This expedient was due to delay in the repair of the tenders normally coupled with these two engines. Note tender has not been repainted and British Railways can be discerned. Both quickly regained their own 2640 gallons type. Brimsdown.

(below) Until 1926 tenders did not have any coal guard or rails on their outer edge. No.7683 was in this form until December 1927.

7924 cont./
Str. 1/11—6/12/35.**G.**
Str. 6/8—12/10/39.**G.**
Str. 4/12/42—16/1/43.**G.**
Str. 1—25/4/45.**G.**
Str. 6/4—29/5/47.**G.**

BOILERS:
924.
924 17/3/02.
2504 29/10/14.
568 15/3/28.
2554 5/9/30.
2579 6/4/33.
2567 6/12/35.
2391 12/10/39.
2363 16/1/43.
2383 25/4/45.

SHEDS:
Colchester.
Ipswich 26/5/34.
Bury St Edmunds 5/6/38.
Cambridge 5/5/40.
Stratford 15/12/40.
Cambridge 3/2/41.

RENUMBERED:
7924 17/6/25.
5413 11/8/46.

CONDEMNED: 20/11/50.
Cut up at Stratford.

_____

7925

Stratford.

To traffic 12/1891.

REPAIRS:
Str. 25/4—22/7/13.**G.**
Str. 27/6—7/2/20.**G.**
Str. 2/7—18/9/23.**G.**
Str. 3/9—17/11/25.**G.**
Str. 13/3—8/6/28.**G.**
Coal guard on tender.
Str. 11/4—30/5/30.**G.**
Str. 22/9—7/10/32.**G.**
Str. 2/2—9/3/36.**G.**
Str. 25/5—19/8/39.**G.**
Str. 22/11—13/12/41.**G.**
Str. 16/7—12/8/44.**G.**
Str. 23/6—18/8/46.**G.**

BOILERS:
925.
925 22/7/13.
512 7/2/20.
2549 17/11/25.
2537 30/5/30.
2575 7/10/32.
2557 9/3/36.
2561 19/8/39.

2545 13/12/41.
2576 12/8/44.
2780 18/8/46.

SHEDS:
Colchester.
Stratford 25/9/39.
Colchester 3/12/39.

RENUMBERED:
7925 17/11/25.
5414 23/12/46.

CONDEMNED: 7/11/49.
Cut up at Stratford.

_____

7926

Stratford.

To traffic 12/1891.

REPAIRS:
Str. 24/7—22/11/01.**G.**
Str. 29/9—20/2/17.**G.**
Records missing.
Str. ?/?—?/8/24.**G.**
Str. 18/2—17/6/25.**G.**
Str. ?/?—?/3/29.**G.**
Coal guard on tender.
Str. 20/5—11/6/31.**G.**
Str. 26/9—13/10/33.**G.**
Str. 25/3—8/4/36.**G.**
Str. ?/?—6/9/39.**G.**
Str. ?/?—1/1/41.**L.**
Str. ?/?—26/2/42.**G.**
Str. ?/?—27/7/44.**G.**
Str. 4—18/1/47.**G.**
Str. 14/5/49. *Not repaired.*

BOILERS:
926.
926 22/11/01.
2519 20/2/17.
2536 ?/8/24.
2504 17/6/25.
2556 ?/3/29.
2570 11/6/31.
2743 13/10/33.
2576 8/4/36.
2569 6/9/39.
2576 26/2/42.
2785 27/7/44.
3358 18/1/47.

SHEDS:
Colchester.
Ipswich 26/5/34.

RENUMBERED:
7926 ?/8/24.
5415 18/8/46.

CONDEMNED: 16/5/49.
Cut up at Stratford.

_____

7927

Stratford.

To traffic 12/1891.

REPAIRS:
Str. 2/5—1/11/04.**G.**
Str. 28/1—3/6/21.**G.**
Pbo. 13/10—25/11/22.**H.**
Str. 11/4—11/9/25.**G.**
*Parry boiler tube cleaner
to Dwg. no.25516 fitted.*
Str. 19/9—29/12/27.**G.**
*Tube cleaner removed.
Coal guard on tender.*
Str. 20/1—1/3/30.**G.**
Str. 1—23/9/32.**G.**
Str. 26/9—30/10/35.**G.**
Str. 1/9—16/10/40.**G.**
Str. 29/11/43—1/1/44.**G.**
Str. 1/6—28/7/46.**G.**
Str. 29/1—13/4/47.**L.**
Str. 19/12/49. *Not repaired.*

BOILERS:
927.
927 1/11/04.
649 3/6/21.
2514 29/12/27.
570 1/3/30.
2791 23/9/32.
2784 30/10/35.
2552 16/10/40.
3301 1/1/44.
2550 28/7/46.

SHEDS:
Colchester.
New England 14/6/34.
March 24/11/34.
New England 26/11/35.
March 17/11/36.
King's Lynn 11/10/39.

RENUMBERED:
7927 11/9/25.
5416 10/11/46.

CONDEMNED: 19/12/49.
Cut up at Stratford.

_____

7928

Stratford.

To traffic 12/1891.

REPAIRS:
Str. 20/6—6/11/05.**G.**

Str. 19/4—18/8/16.**G.**
Cam. 24/5—21/8/23.**H.**
Str. 30/1—1/5/25.**G.**
Str. 9/9—14/12/27.**G.**
Coal guard on tender.
Str. 12/6—29/7/30.**G.**
Str. 25/5—16/6/33.**G.**
Str. 29/1—25/2/36.**G.**
Str. 21/1—24/2/40.**G.**
Str. 18/12/42—12/2/43.**G.**
Str. 25/3—15/4/44.**L.**
Str. 2—21/9/45.**G.**
Str. 11/6—30/7/48.**G.**
Str. 11—28/7/50.**C/H.**
Str. 27/3—5/5/52.**G.**

BOILERS:
928.
928 6/11/05.
640 18/8/16.
2530 1/5/25.
2576 29/7/30.
3302 16/6/33.
2779 25/2/36.
2788 24/2/40.
3341 12/2/43.
3345 21/9/45.
3375 30/7/48.
3323 28/7/50.
23549 5/5/52.

SHEDS:
Cambridge .
March 25/10/31.
Cambridge 6/12/31.
March 23/2/35.
King's Lynn 2/10/36.
March 24/1/37.
Norwich 24/3/37.
Stratford 13/12/40.
Norwich 6/2/41.
Yarmouth Beach 14/3/43.
Norwich 20/8/44.
Melton Constable 2/3/47.
Norwich 19/4/47.
Melton Constable 14/1/48.
Norwich 24/3/48.

RENUMBERED:
7928 1/5/25.
5417 17/11/46.
65417 30/7/48.

CONDEMNED: 20/8/56.
Cut up at Stratford.

_____

7929

Stratford.

To traffic 12/1891.

REPAIRS:
Str. ?/?—?/6/05.**G.**

7929 cont./
Str. 19/7—7/10/15.**G.**
Str. 10/5—12/10/22.**G.**
Records missing.
Str. 26/8—19/11/27.**G.**
Coal guard on tender.
Str. 31/1—15/2/30.**G.**
Str. 3—19/5/32.**G.**
Str. 17/7—8/8/35.**G.**
Str. ?/?—10/11/39.**G.**
Str. ?/?—30/1/43.**G.**
Str. 26/5—13/6/45.**G.**
Str. 8/2—12/4/47.**L.**

BOILERS:
 929.
 929 ?/6/05.
 2511 7/10/15.
  507 12/10/22.
 2507 19/11/27.
 2540 15/2/30.
 2776 19/5/32.
 2786 8/8/35.
 2556 10/11/39.
 3340 30/1/43.
 3306 13/6/45.

SHEDS:
Cambridge .
March 25/10/31.
Cambridge 6/12/31.
March 23/2/35.
New England 19/10/35.
March 14/11/36.
Cambridge 21/11/36.
Stratford 15/12/40.

RENUMBERED:
7929 *by* 25/2/25.
5418 28/7/46.

CONDEMNED: 12/3/48.
Cut up at Stratford.

7930

Stratford.

To traffic 12/1891.

REPAIRS:
Str. 16/2—2/9/04.**G.**
Str. 22/2—14/6/18.**G.**
Str. 17/6—12/9/24.**G.**
Str. ?/?—?/12/28.**G.**
Coal guard on tender.
Str. 16/6—8/7/31.**G.**

BOILERS:
 930.
 930 2/9/04.
 2531 14/6/18.
 2559 12/9/24.
 2542 ?/12/28.

2524 8/7/31.

SHEDS:
Peterborough East.
New England 27/4/34.
Peterborough East 26/10/34.

RENUMBERED:
7930 12/9/24.

CONDEMNED: 5/1/35.

7931

Stratford.

To traffic 1/1892.

REPAIRS:
Str. 28/8—6/12/12.**G.**
Str. 13/2—11/5/17.**G.**
Str. ?/?—?/6/20.**G.**
Str. 4/8—20/10/23.**G.**
Str. 26/9—9/12/25.**G.**
Str. 8/12/27—17/3/28.**G.**
Coal guard on tender.
Str. 13/2—5/4/30.**G.**
Str. 11/8—5/9/32.**G.**
Str. 18/1—21/2/36.**G.**
Str. 14/12/40—4/1/41.**G.**
Str. 12/3—13/4/44.**G.**
Str. 29/9—23/10/46.**G.**
Str. 27/1/50. *Not repaired.*

BOILERS:
 931.
 931 6/12/12.
 517 11/5/17.
 564 ?/6/20.
 931 9/12/25.
 2514 5/4/30.
 2557 5/9/32.
 2579 21/2/36.
 2741 4/1/41.
 3331 13/4/44.
 3383 23/10/46.

SHEDS:
Peterborough East.
New England 26/3/36.
Doncaster 17/10/42.
March 31/10/42.
Norwich 26/2/48.

RENUMBERED:
7931 9/12/25.
5419 9/12/46.

CONDEMNED: 6/2/50.
Cut up at Stratford.

7932

Stratford.

To traffic 1/1892.

REPAIRS:
Str. ?/?—?/12/06.**G.**
Str. 8/6—29/9/16.**G.**
Str. ?/?—?/2/20.**G.**
Str. 9/5—26/8/22.**G.**
Str. 6/11/24—31/1/25.**G.**
Str. 3/9—9/12/26.**G.**
Str. 5/3—30/4/29.**G.**
Coal guard on tender.
Str. 20/3—29/5/31.**G.**
Str. 19/9—6/10/33.**G.**
Str. 22/3—28/4/36.**G.**
Str. 20/3—4/5/40.**G.**
Str. 2/1—11/3/44.**G.**
Str. 14/7—25/8/46.**G.**
Str. 23/8—10/9/48.**H.**
Spark arrestor fitted.
Str. 22/4—6/5/50.**G.**
Str. 18/11—12/12/52.**C/L.**
Str. 4/2—7/3/53.**G.**
Str. 20/10—16/11/57.**G.**

BOILERS:
 932.
 932 ?/12/06.
 2518 29/9/16.
 513 ?/2/20.
 2531 31/1/25.
 551 30/4/29.
 2572 29/5/31.
 2571 6/10/33.
 2568 28/4/36.
 2565 4/5/40.
 2764 11/3/44.
 3301 25/8/46.
 3369 10/9/48.
 3387 6/5/50.
 3387 reno.23571 12/12/52.
 23541 7/3/53.
 23579 16/11/57.

SHEDS:
Stratford.
March 30/11/27.
Stratford 22/6/28.
March 13/10/28.
Cambridge 9/6/36.
Bury St Edmunds 10/12/39.
Cambridge 11/7/45.
Bury St Edmunds 13/6/47.
March 16/6/57.
New England 30/4/61.
March 12/11/61.
Stratford 17/6/62.

RENUMBERED:
7932 31/1/25.
5420 16/8/46.
65420 10/9/48.

CONDEMNED: 1/8/62.
*Sold for scrap to J. Cashmore,
Great Bridge, 11/62.*

7933

Stratford.

To traffic 1/1892.

REPAIRS:
Str. 1/10/09—1/3/10.**G.**
Str. 13/5—18/8/21.**G.**
Str. 26/6—7/11/23.**G.**
Str. 1/12/25—26/2/26.**G.**
Str. ?/?—?/9/28.**G.**
Coal guard on tender.
Str. 30/3—23/4/31.**G.**
Str. ?/?—10/11/33.**G.**

BOILERS:
 933.
 933 1/3/10.
 2506 18/8/21.
 2534 7/11/23.
 2524 26/2/26.
 2748 23/4/31.
 3310 10/11/33.

SHEDS:
Ipswich.
Norwich 11/10/33.
Ipswich by 1/1/35.

RENUMBERED:
7933 26/2/26.

CONDEMNED: 21/3/36.

7934

Stratford.

To traffic 1/1892.

REPAIRS:
Str. ?/?—?/6/03.**G.**
Str. 28/7—12/10/15.**G.**
Str. 14/6—24/10/18.**G.**
Str. 16/11/22—9/2/23.**G.**
Str. 26/4—31/7/28.**G.**
Coal guard on tender.
Parry soot blower fitted.
Str. 18/2—7/3/31.**G.**
Parry soot blower removed.
Str. 6—27/10/33.**G.**
Str. 23/4—8/5/36.**G.**
Str. ?/?—?/11/39.**G.**
Str. ?/?—?/6/43.**G.**
Str. 22—29/9/45.**G.**
Str. 28/2/48. *Not repaired.*

Between 1926 and 1932, those which received a major repair had coal guards fitted to the top edge on each side of the tender. These guards had a half-round beading to the edge of the plate.

On the left hand side of the tender there was a short plate to form a channel for storing the fire irons.

7934 cont./
BOILERS:
934.
934 ?/6/03.
2513 12/10/15.
2508 24/10/18.
511 9/2/23.
2504 31/7/28.
2516 7/3/31.
2578 27/10/33.
2788 8/5/36.
2557 ?/11/39.
2750 ?/6/43.
3375 29/9/45.

SHED:
Ipswich.

RENUMBERED:
7934 ?/?
5421 18/8/46.

CONDEMNED: 17/3/48.
Cut up at Stratford.

7936

Stratford.

To traffic 8/1892.

REPAIRS:
Str. 14/5—11/11/02.**G.**
Str. 6/1—11/5/15.**G.**
Str. 25/1—21/6/18.**G.**
Str. 6/5—10/8/21.**G.**
Str. 17/1—10/4/24.**G.**
Str. ?/?—?/7/29.**G.**
Coal guard on tender.
Str. 18/12/31—8/1/32.**G.**
Str. 20/9—5/10/34.**G.**

BOILERS:
936.
936 11/11/02.
2508 11/5/15.
514 21/6/18.
2514 10/8/21.
922 10/4/24.
2510 ?/7/29.
2519 8/1/32.
2726 5/10/34.

SHEDS:
Ipswich.
Norwich ?/?/?.
Lowestoft 7/4/34.
Norwich 5/5/34.
Ipswich 9/6/34.

RENUMBERED:
7936 10/4/24.

CONDEMNED: 22/4/37.

7937

Stratford.

To traffic 8/1892.

REPAIRS:
Str. ?/?—?/6/06.**G.**
Str. 17/8/17—11/1/18.**G.**
Str. 1/8—31/12/22.**G.**
Str. 1/12/24—6/2/25.**G.**
Str. 6/5—3/9/27.**G.**
Coal guard on tender.
Str. 29/8—5/10/29.**G.**
Str. 31/5—25/6/32.**G.**
Str. 27/7—19/9/34.**G.**
Str. 18/7—27/8/37.**G.**
Str. 23/9—27/10/41.**G.**
Str. 16/1—15/2/44.**G.**
Str. 20/2—5/3/45.**L.**
Str. 11/12/45—9/1/46.**G.**
Str. 6/8—1/9/48.**G.**
Str. 2/3—10/4/52.**G.**
Str. 23/4—9/5/52.**C/L.**
Str. 27/5/55. *Not repaired.*

BOILERS:
937.
937 ?/6/06.
931 11/1/18.
2511 31/12/22.
2541 3/9/27.
921 5/10/29.
2540 25/6/32.
2531 19/9/34.
2545 27/8/37.
2562 27/10/41.
2574 15/2/44.
3313 9/1/46.
3341 1/9/48.
23548 10/4/52.

SHEDS:
Ipswich.
Parkeston 20/2/28.
Ipswich 21/4/28.
Norwich 28/3/40.
Ipswich 18/3/51.
March 10/8/52.

RENUMBERED:
7937 6/2/25.
5422 8/12/46.
65422 28/8/48.

CONDEMNED: 4/7/55.
Cut up at Stratford.

7938

Stratford.

To traffic 8/1892.

REPAIRS:
Str. 7/6—4/11/09.**G.**
Str. 10/7—28/10/14.**G.**
Str. 9/3—3/6/20.**G.**
Str. 5/8—5/11/24.**G.**
Str. ?/?—?/6/29.**G.**
Coal guard on tender.
Str. 22/7—21/8/31.**G.**

BOILERS:
938.
938 4/11/09.
895 28/10/14.
515 3/6/20.
2531 ?/6/29.
2513 21/8/31.

SHED:
Stratford.

RENUMBERED:
7938 5/11/24.

CONDEMNED: 29/10/34.

7939

Stratford.

To traffic 8/1892.

REPAIRS:
Str. 25/7—11/12/03.**G.**
Str. 31/1—30/4/19.**G.**
Str. 15/3—3/10/22.**G.**
Str. 19/1—19/4/24.**G.**
Str. ?/?—?/10/26.**G.**
Str. ?/?—?/10/28.**G.**
Coal guard on tender.
Str. 10—30/4/31.**G.**
Str. 13—26/7/33.**G.**

BOILERS:
939.
939 11/12/03.
938 30/4/19.
2535 3/10/22.
2513 19/4/24.
933 ?/10/26.
2572 ?/10/28.
2552 30/4/31.
2565 26/7/33.

SHEDS:
Ipswich.
Cambridge 26/10/34.
Ipswich 3/11/34.

RENUMBERED:
7939 19/4/24.

CONDEMNED: 7/2/36.

7940

Stratford.

To traffic 8/1892.

REPAIRS:
Str. 10/12/02—25/6/03.**G.**
Str. 6/4—21/7/16.**G.**
Str. 15/2—4/7/23.**G.**
Str. 19/3—13/6/25.**G.**
Str. 12/8—29/10/27.**G.**
Coal guard on tender.
Str. 10/1—15/2/30.**G.**
Str. 13/10—2/11/32.**G.**
Str. 11/4—4/6/35.**G.**
Str. 25/7—19/9/39.**G.**
Str. 23/3—29/4/42.**G.**
Str. 7/5—8/6/44.**G.**
Str. 15—29/6/44.**L.**
Str. 23/11—18/12/45.**L.**
Str. 24/11—20/12/46.**G.**

BOILERS:
940.
940 25/6/03.
567 21/7/16.
2524 4/7/23.
2526 13/6/25.
2539 15/2/30.
2742 2/11/32.
3328 4/6/35.
3310 19/9/39.
2569 29/4/42.
3350 8/6/44.
3349 20/12/46.

SHED:
Ipswich.

RENUMBERED:
7940 13/6/25.
5423 13/12/46.

CONDEMNED: 20/11/50.
Cut up at Stratford.

7941

Stratford.

To traffic 8/1892.

REPAIRS:
Str. 8/7—13/11/03.**G.**
Str. 9/2—29/5/14.**G.**
Str. 21/5—10/9/20.**G.**
Str. 20/9—13/2/23.**G.**
Str. 31/3—19/4/23.**L.**
Str. 2/9—20/11/25.**G.**
Str. 29/2—31/5/28.**G.**
Coal guard on tender.
Str. 19/6—22/8/30.**G.**
Str. 3—23/12/32.**G.**

7941 cont./
Str. 27/4—5/5/33.**L**.
Vac. brake & steam heat added.
Str. 4/6—12/7/34.**L**.
Cab altered.
Str. 15/6—20/7/35.**G**.
Str. 4—27/8/37.**G**.
Str. 3/7—8/9/39.**G**.
Str. 30/10—29/11/41.**G**.
Str. 18/11/43—1/1/44.**G**.
Str. 29/12/45—25/1/46.**G**.
Str. 19/2—24/3/49.**G**.
Str. 14—29/9/51.**G**.
Str. 22/2—20/3/54.**G**.
Str. 15/2—17/5/56.**G**.

BOILERS:
941.
941 13/11/03.
2500 29/5/14.
2546 10/9/20.
2505 31/5/28.
2527 22/8/30.
2549 23/12/32.
2524 20/7/35.
3318 27/8/37.
3323 8/9/39.
2758 29/11/41.
2767 25/1/46.
3377 24/3/49.
23530 29/9/51.
23523 20/3/54.
23572 17/5/56.

SHEDS:
Ipswich.
Colchester 15/11/34.
Bury St Edmunds 5/6/38.
Cambridge 10/12/39.
Colchester 3/6/44.
Stratford 6/12/59.

RENUMBERED:
7941 20/11/25.
5424 16/6/46.
65424 19/3/49.

CONDEMNED: 18/12/59.
Cut up at Stratford.

_____

7942

Stratford.

To traffic 9/1892.

REPAIRS:
Str. 9/9/04—17/2/05.**G**.
Str. 22/8—31/12/19.**G**.
Str. 9/11/23—1/3/24.**G**.
Str. 19/3—26/6/26.**G**.
Coal guard on tender.
Str. 23/2—6/6/28.**G**.
Str. 28/4—4/7/30.**G**.

Str. 22/9—14/10/32.**G**.
Str. 14/11—13/12/35.**G**.
Str. 9/11—22/12/39.**G**.
Str. 24/2—10/4/43.**G**.
Str. 16/12/45—12/1/46.**G**.
Str. 28/1—9/2/48.**L**.
Str. 13/2—15/3/49.**G**.
Str. 26/12/50—18/1/51.**C/H**.
Str. 28/12/52—7/1/53.**C/L**.
Str. 18/2—23/3/53.**G**.
Str. 20/9/56. *Not repaired.*

BOILERS:
942.
942 17/2/05.
2538 31/12/19.
2556 1/3/24.
2534 26/6/26.
2568 6/6/28.
2569 4/7/30.
2521 14/10/32.
2747 13/12/35.
2790 22/12/39.
3347 10/4/43.
2773 12/1/46.
3372 15/3/49.
23508 18/1/51.
23575 23/3/53.

SHEDS:
Ipswich.
Colchester 11/4/29.
King's Lynn 28/5/39.
Cambridge 2/10/49.

RENUMBERED:
Still **942** *at* 1/3/24.
7942 26/6/26.
5425 2/1/47.
65425 12/3/49.

CONDEMNED: 1/10/56.
Cut up at Stratford.

_____

7943

Stratford.

To traffic 9/1892.

REPAIRS:
Str. 30/3—14/10/04.**G**.
Str. 7/2—21/5/19.**G**.
Str. 26/10/23—12/1/24.**G**.
Str. 22/1—30/4/26.**G**.
Coal guard on tender.
Str. 28/1—16/3/28.**G**.
Str. 4/7—22/8/30.**G**.
Str. 28/11—20/12/32.**G**.
Str. 16/8—20/9/35.**G**.
Str. 16/7—27/9/39.**G**.
Str. 7/9—19/10/40.**G**.
Str. 8/8—17/9/43.**G**.
Str. 8—28/7/45.**G**.

Str. 9/6—28/7/48.**G**.
Str. 27/4/51. *Not repaired.*

BOILERS:
943.
943 14/10/04.
525 21/5/19.
2550 30/4/26.
2565 16/3/28.
2579 22/8/30.
2569 20/12/32.
2785 20/9/35.
2789 19/10/40.
2781 17/9/43.
2374 28/7/45.
3376 28/7/48.

SHEDS:
Ipswich.
Colchester 26/4/29.
Ipswich 11/5/37.
Norwich 28/3/40.
Stratford 13/12/40.
Norwich 3/2/41.
Yarmouth 27/11/46.
Norwich 2/2/47.
Yarmouth Beach 23/2/47.
Norwich 23/3/47.

RENUMBERED:
7943 30/4/26.
5426 26/8/46.
65426 24/7/48.

CONDEMNED: 21/5/51.
Cut up at Stratford.

_____

7944

Stratford.

To traffic 9/1892.

REPAIRS:
Str. 23/3—21/10/09.**G**.
Str. 22/6—31/10/17.**G**.
Str. 28/11/19—5/3/20.**G**.
Str. 16/6—31/10/22.**G**.
Str. 6/8—16/11/27.**G**.
Coal guard on tender.
Str. 4—23/10/29.**G**.
Str. 1—19/12/31.**G**.

BOILERS:
944.
944 21/10/09.
920 31/10/17.
925 5/3/20.
2502 31/10/22.
2529 16/11/27.
2541 23/10/29.
2559 19/12/31.

SHEDS:
Parkeston.
Ipswich 15/11/34.

RENUMBERED:
7944 ?/?

CONDEMNED: 12/2/35.

_____

7945

Stratford.

To traffic 11/1892.

REPAIRS:
Str. 13/9/05—9/1/06.**G**.
Str. 14/5—28/8/20.**G**.
Ips. 30/8—28/11/22.**H**.
Str. 16/2—3/7/25.**G**.
Str. 5/8—28/10/27.**G**.
Coal guard on tender.
Str. 26/7—14/9/29.**G**.
Str. 14/10—11/12/31.**G**.
Str. 31/1—19/2/32.**H**.
Str. 16/5—16/7/34.**G**.
Str. 27/7—10/9/37.**G**.
Str. 23/12/40—31/1/41.**G**.
Str. 27/8—23/9/44.**G**.
Str. 4—27/10/45.**G**.
Str. 23/5—1/7/47.**G**.

BOILERS:
945.
945 9/1/06.
2544 28/8/20.
2520 14/9/29.
519 11/12/31.
569 16/7/34.
2746 10/9/37.
2776 31/1/41.
2559 23/9/44.
2395 1/7/47.

SHEDS:
Parkeston.
Stratford 19/12/41.
Colchester 1/1/50.

RENUMBERED:
7945 3/7/25.
5427 13/1/47.

CONDEMNED: 23/10/50.
Cut up at Stratford.

_____

7507

Stratford.

To traffic 5/1899.

7507 cont./
REPAIRS:
Str. 9/8—13/10/10.**G.**
Str. 12/5—16/9/17.**G.**
Str. 19/11/20—10/2/21.**G.**
Str. 16/9—3/12/24.**G.**
Str. ?/?—?/5/29.**G.**
Str. 18/8—4/9/31.**G.**
Coal guard on tender.

BOILERS:
 507.
 507 13/10/10.
 649 16/9/17.
2551 10/2/21.
2519 3/12/24.
2547 ?/5/29.
2515 4/9/31.

SHEDS:
Stratford.
March 28/9/27.
King's Lynn 10/7/33.

RENUMBERED:
7507 3/12/24.

CONDEMNED: 15/1/35.

7508

Stratford.

To traffic 5/1899.

REPAIRS:
Str. 23/12/14—12/3/15.**G.**

Str. 14/4—24/10/23.**G.**
Str. 11/7—30/9/25.**G.**
Str. 21/2—14/6/28.**G.**
Coal guard on tender.
Str. 2/7—22/8/30.**G.**
Str. 27/6—14/7/33.**G.**
Str. 21/1—21/2/36.**G.**
Str. 13/6—8/8/40.**G.**
Str. 4/6—12/7/44.**G.**
Str. 26/10—29/11/46.**G.**

BOILERS:
 508.
2507 12/3/15.
2503 24/10/23.
2577 22/8/30.
2576 14/7/33.
2552 21/2/36.
2727 8/8/40.
3354 12/7/44.
3386 29/11/46.

SHEDS:
Cambridge.
Stratford 24/6/26.
Cambridge 22/10/26.
Stratford 11/6/27.
Cambridge 28/9/27.
Peterborough East 11/10/28.
March 1/9/29.
Cambridge 21/9/36.
New England 30/7/38.
March 15/5/41.
New England 28/6/41.
Doncaster 17/10/42.
Mexborough 24/10/42.
Melton Constable 16/4/43.
Stratford 23/4/43.

Ipswich 2/5/47.

RENUMBERED:
7508 30/9/25.
5428 23/11/46.

CONDEMNED: 1/8/49.
Cut up at Stratford.

7509

Stratford.

To traffic 5/1899.

REPAIRS:
Str. ?/?—?/6/08.**G.**
Str. 7/11/17—15/3/18.**G.**
Str. 28/7—16/11/23.**G.**
Str. 15/6—13/8/25.**G.**
Str. 27/1—3/5/28.**G.**
Coal guard on tender.
Str. 12/3—2/5/30.**G.**
Str. 30/8—26/9/32.**G.**
Str. 5—8/10/32.**H.**
After collision.
Str. 19/12/36—18/3/37.**G.**
Str. 21/3—29/5/40.**G.**
Str. 29/11—23/12/41.**L.**
Str. 3/2—26/3/43.**G.**
Str. 4—22/3/45.**G.**
Str. 1/4—12/6/47.**G.**

BOILERS:
 509.
 509 ?/6/08.
 521 15/3/18.

2545 3/5/28.
2742 2/5/30.
2544 26/9/32.
2390 18/3/37.
2382 29/5/40.
2360 26/3/43.
2344 22/3/45.
2774 12/6/47.

SHEDS:
Cambridge.
Stratford 22/6/26.
Cambridge 22/10/26.
Stratford 11/6/27.
Cambridge 28/9/27.
Peterborough East 10/10/28.
March 1/9/29.
New England 23/10/33.
Parkeston 13/3/35.
Ipswich 22/4/36.

RENUMBERED:
7509 13/8/25.
5429 15/12/46.

CONDEMNED: 13/11/50.
Cut up at Stratford.

(below) **From 1926 this side of the tender also got a full length solid coping to the outer edge. Southend, 24th August 1929.**

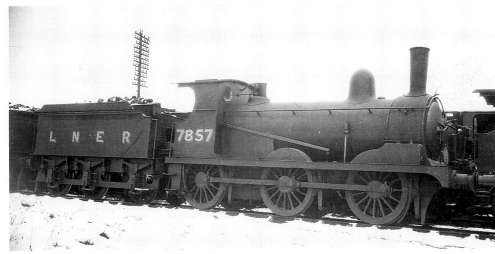

No explanation has been found why in 1931/2 No.7857's tender had two pipes mounted below the coal guard on the right hand side for the full length.

(above) Tenders originally with engines built before 1899 had a short vertical handrail at the front end. Stratford shed.

Tenders built from 1899 on, and those re-conditioned for use with later engines, had a taller rail to match the cab cut-out of the engines built from that year onwards. Here we have such a tender paired with an engine with the original style of cabside cut out..

7510

Stratford.

To traffic 5/1899.

REPAIRS:
Str. 12/1—3/4/11.**G.**
Str. 26/6/22—11/1/23.**G.**
Str. 18/10—28/11/24.**G.**
Str. 25/6—28/10/27.**G.**
Coal guard on tender.
Str. 19/9—19/10/29.**G.**
Str. 27/8—17/10/31.**G.**
Str. 6/7—23/8/34.**G.**
Str. 10/10—27/11/36.**G.**
Str. 11/3—10/5/40.**G.**
Str. 4/7—31/8/43.**G.**
Str. 7—20/10/45.**G.**
Str. 15/8—14/9/48.**G.**
Str. 26/8—16/9/49.**C/H.**
Str. 9/6—2/8/52.**G.**

BOILERS:
510.
510 3/4/11.
2564 28/10/27.
2532 19/10/29.
2741 17/10/31.
2382 27/11/36.
2781 10/5/40.
2575 31/8/43.
3377 20/10/45.
2788 14/9/48.
2773 16/9/49.
23559 2/8/52.

SHEDS:
Cambridge.
Norwich 23/6/30.
March 29/8/30.
Cambridge 25/9/32.
Ipswich 25/2/33.
Stratford 13/12/40.
Ipswich 4/11/41.

RENUMBERED:
7510 28/11/24.
5430 17/11/46.
65430 11/9/48.

CONDEMNED: 2/1/56.
Cut up at Stratford.

7511

Stratford.

To traffic 5/1899.

REPAIRS:
Str. 31/8—4/12/11.**G.**
Str. 22/7—21/12/22.**G.**
Str. 3/2—10/8/23.**G.**
Str. 14/3—3/7/25.**G.**
Str. 7/7—22/9/27.**G.**
Str. 5/9—2/10/29.**G.**
Coal guard on tender.
Str. 19/8—2/10/31.**G.**
Str. 11/6—27/7/34.**G.**
Str. 5/8—6/9/37.**G.**
Str. 31/3—1/5/41.**G.**
Str. 13/8—26/10/44.**G.**
Str. 20/2—27/4/48.**G.**

BOILERS:
511.
511 4/12/11.
931 21/12/22.
2501 3/7/25.
641 22/9/27.
2538 2/10/29.
2547 2/10/31.
2551 27/7/34.
2531 6/9/37.
3309 1/5/41.
3360 26/10/44.
2769 27/4/48.

SHEDS:
Cambridge.
Stratford 23/6/26.
Cambridge 21/10/26.
Norwich 23/6/30.
March 29/8/30.
Cambridge 23/2/35.
Ipswich 30/9/35.
Parkeston 7/6/36.
Stratford 12/7/47.
Colchester 4/9/49.

RENUMBERED:
7511 3/7/25.
5431 19/11/46.
65431 24/4/48.

CONDEMNED: 5/3/51.
Cut up at Stratford.

7512

Stratford.

To traffic 6/1899.

REPAIRS:
Str. 12/1—7/4/11.**G.**
Str. 22/8—31/12/19.**G.**
Str. 11/4—9/8/21.**G.**
Str. 28/12/22—4/4/23.**G.**
Str. 7/11—30/12/24.**G.**
Str. 26/5—2/9/27.**G.**
Coal guard on tender.
Str. 14/8—28/9/29.**G.**
Str. 26/8—12/10/31.**G.**
Str. 10/12/34—11/1/35.**G.**
Cab altered. Vacuum brake and steam heat fitted.

Str. 4/4—18/5/37.**G.**
Str. 23/7—27/9/39.**G.**
Str. 18/10—8/11/41.**G.**
Str. 27/11—3/12/41.**L.**
Str. 13/8—15/9/44.**G.**
Str. 28/3—19/5/47.**G.**
Str. 7/11—2/12/48.**G.**
Str. 20/11—16/12/50.**G.**
Str. 27/10—29/11/52.**G.**
Str. 16/6—29/7/55.**G.**

BOILERS:
512.
512 7/4/11.
2513 31/12/19.
927 9/8/21.
516 4/4/23.
922 28/9/29.
2518 12/10/31.
2528 11/1/35.
2576 27/9/39.
2355 8/11/41.
3323 15/9/44.
3329 19/5/47.
3342 2/12/48.
23506 16/12/50.
23569 29/11/52.
23547 29/7/55.

SHEDS:
March.
Cambridge 26/1/35.
Colchester 3/6/44.

RENUMBERED:
7512 30/12/24.
5432 8/9/46.
65432 27/11/48.

CONDEMNED: 10/3/58.
Cut up at Stratford.

7514

Stratford.

To traffic 5/1899.

REPAIRS:
Str. 14/1—31/5/12.**G.**
Str. 7/12/17—30/4/18.**G.**
Str. 19/12/23—25/3/24.**G.**
Str. 19/3—16/7/26.**G.**
Str. 11/8—12/10/28.**G.**
Coal guard on tender.
Str. 7/12/30—2/1/31.**G.**
Str. 18/12/33—12/1/34.**G.**
Str. 5/7—12/8/37.**G.**
Str. 19/6—1/8/41.**G.**
Str. 29/8—29/9/44.**G.**
Str. 25/2—15/4/47.**G.**
Str. 12—23/2/50.**G.**
Str. 8—28/11/53.**G.**
Str. 30/12/57. *Not repaired.*

BOILERS:
514.
514 31/5/12.
509 30/4/18.
526 2/1/31.
3318 12/1/34.
2356 12/8/37.
2383 1/8/41.
846 29/9/44.
2785 15/4/47.
2579 23/2/50.
23520 28/11/53.

SHEDS:
Stratford.
Norwich 4/1/29.
Lowestoft 1/1/35.
Norwich 15/1/35.
Lowestoft 25/5/35.
Norwich 2/5/37.
Lowestoft 6/11/38.
Ipswich 13/12/41.
March 21/10/42.
Norwich 1/1/49.
Lowestoft 5/6/49.
Ipswich 25/3/56.

RENUMBERED:
7514 25/3/24.
5433 10/11/46.
65433 23/2/50.

CONDEMNED: 13/1/58.
Cut up at Stratford.

7515

Stratford.

To traffic 6/1899.

REPAIRS:
Str. 27/1—30/5/12.**G.**
Str. 23/1—9/4/20.**G.**
Str. 20/3—19/10/22.**G.**
Str. 3/4—25/7/25.**G.**
Str. 23/6—7/10/27.**G.**
Str. 10/10—9/11/29.**G.**
Coal guard on tender.
Str. 4/6—9/7/32.**G.**
Str. 29/5—12/7/35.**G.**
Str. 13/5—14/6/40.**G.**
Str. 25/4—2/6/43.**G.**
Str. 15/6—4/8/44.**G.**
Str. 9/3—4/4/47.**G.**
Str. 1—14/1/50.**G.**
Str. 12/4—14/5/54.**G.**

BOILERS:
515.
515 30/5/12.
2501 9/4/20.
2528 25/7/25.
516 9/11/29.

7515 cont./
2786 9/7/32.
2742 12/7/35.
2572 14/6/40.
3332 4/8/44.
3309 4/4/47.
3381 14/1/50.
23518 14/5/54.

SHEDS:
Stratford.
Ipswich 8/10/27.
Norwich 24/10/32.
Lowestoft 9/9/33.
Norwich 25/5/35.
New England 28/10/35.
Grantham 14/2/36.
New England 29/4/36.
March 6/5/41.
New England 30/6/41.
Doncaster 17/10/42.
Mexborough 24/10/42.
Stratford 2/6/43.
Parkeston 10/7/49.
Colchester 1/1/50.
Stratford 8/1/50.
Parkeston 17/6/50.

RENUMBERED:
7515 25/7/25.
5434 23/11/46.
65434 14/1/50.

CONDEMNED: 16/11/59.
Cut up at Stratford.

7516

Stratford.

To traffic 6/1899.

REPAIRS:
Str. 18/2—12/7/10.**G.**
Str. 2/11/22—17/2/23.**G.**
Str. 3/4—5/6/25.**G.**
Str. 7/10/27—10/1/28.**G.**
Coal guard on tender.
Str. 14/5—27/6/30.**G.**
Str. 22/5—16/6/33.**G.**
Str. 22/6—24/7/36.**G.**
Str. 14/10—1/12/39.**G.**
Str. 20/4—16/6/43.**G.**
Str. 15/7—3/8/45.**G.**
Str. 28/6—17/8/48.**G.**
Str. 21/7—22/8/52.**G.**
Str. 26/9/56. *Not repaired.*

BOILERS:
516.
516 12/7/10.
944 17/2/23.
2554 10/1/28.
649 27/6/30.

2527 16/6/33.
2575 24/7/36.
2567 1/12/39.
2547 16/6/43.
3371 3/8/45.
3319 17/8/48.
23561 22/8/52.

SHEDS:
Stratford.
Norwich 4/1/29.
Yarmouth 13/10/34.
Norwich 15/12/34.
Lowestoft 19/9/43.
Norwich 28/12/47.
Lowestoft 4/2/48.
Ipswich 7/8/55.

RENUMBERED:
7516 5/6/25.
5435 1/9/46.
65435 14/8/48.

CONDEMNED: 15/10/56.
Cut up at Stratford.

7517

Stratford.

To traffic 6/1899.

REPAIRS:
Str. 11/2—28/6/10.**G.**
Str. 1/9—20/2/17.**G.**
Str. 25/10/22—26/5/23.**G.**
Str. 2/4—17/6/25.**G.**
Str. 26/5—2/9/27.**G.**
Coal guard on tender.
Str. 29/11/29—6/1/30.**G.**
Str. 29/1—26/2/30.**L.**
Str. 11/3—8/4/32.**G.**
Str. 18/4—2/6/36.**G.**
Str. 16/4—18/8/39.**G.**
Str. 29/11—26/12/41.**G.**
Str. 30/7—24/8/44.**G.**
Str. 1/9—15/10/46.**G.**
Str. 22/8—6/9/47.**L.**

BOILERS:
517.
517 28/6/10.
2522 20/2/17.
2560 17/6/25.
563 2/9/27.
523 6/1/30.
2563 8/4/32.
2556 2/6/36.
2564 18/8/39.
2570 26/12/41.
2727 24/8/44.
3382 15/10/46.

SHEDS:
Stratford.
Colchester 21/10/27.
Stratford 25/9/39.
Colchester 3/12/39.
Stratford 19/1/46.
Colchester 1/2/48.
Stratford 16/5/48.

RENUMBERED:
7517 17/6/25.
5436 17/11/46.

CONDEMNED: 12/12/49.
Cut up at Stratford.

7518

Stratford.

To traffic 6/1899.

REPAIRS:
Str. 11/2—21/7/09.**G.**
Str. 29/9—20/2/17.**G.**
Str. 10/1—12/7/23.**G.**
Str. 17/9—10/12/27.**G.**
Coal guard on tender.
Str. 19/11—14/12/29.**G.**
Str. 13—29/1/32.**G.**
Str. 31/7—5/9/34.**G.**

BOILERS:
518.
518 21/7/09.
2523 20/2/17.
2520 12/7/23.
2540 10/12/27.
2529 14/12/29.
2775 29/1/32.

SHEDS:
March.
Norwich 20/6/28.
March 7/8/28.
Cambridge 25/9/32.
March 21/4/33.
Cambridge 23/2/35.
Ipswich 30/9/35.

RENUMBERED:
7518 ?/?

CONDEMNED: 15/4/37.

7519

Stratford.

To traffic 6/1899.

REPAIRS:
Str. 18/11/09—6/4/10.**G.**

Str. 7/12/17—23/5/18.**G.**
Str. 7/3—28/6/23.**G.**
Str. 13/10/27—18/1/28.**G.**
Coal guard on tender.
Str. 28/1—15/2/30.**G.**
Str. 23/2—4/3/32.**G.**

BOILERS:
519.
519 6/4/10.
2529 23/5/18.
2509 28/6/23.
2528 15/2/30.
2564 4/3/32.

SHED:
Stratford.

RENUMBERED:
7519 ?/?

CONDEMNED: 19/12/34.

7520

Stratford.

To traffic 6/1899.

REPAIRS:
Str. 28/7—23/11/09.**G.**
Str. 28/7—12/12/16.**G.**
Str. 3/3—28/6/23.**G.**
Str. 14/2—25/3/25.**G.**
Str. 1/9—23/11/27.**G.**
Coal guard on tender.
Str. 21/11—21/12/29.**G.**
Str. 11/8—12/9/30.**G.**
Str. 11/1—6/2/32.**G.**
Str. 4/11—9/12/35.**G.**
Str. 20/7—19/8/38.**G.**
Str. 7—13/9/38.**L.**
Str. 2/7—13/8/41.**G.**
Str. 6/6—15/7/44.**G.**
Str. 5—24/1/47.**G.**

BOILERS:
520.
520 23/11/09.
2521 12/12/16.
2529 28/6/23.
925 23/11/27.
2573 21/12/29.
2750 6/2/32.
2749 9/12/35.
2543 19/8/38.
2726 13/8/41.
3355 15/7/44.
3388 24/1/47.

SHEDS:
Cambridge.
Ipswich 19/6/28.
March 16/10/28.

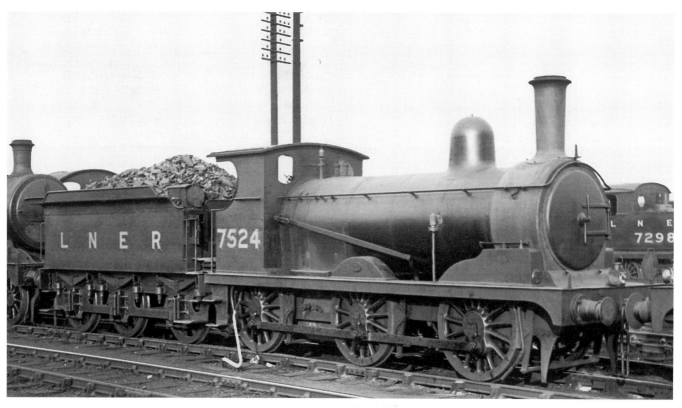

Tender changing led to some with a shallow cab cut-out being paired with a tender having the short vertical handrail.

At Grouping, most were in the 1914 -18 wartime grey paint, without lining, but until their first LNER repair they kept the large brass number plate on the cab side (*see also* page 10). No.597, ex works 22nd September 1923, had its big brass plates replaced by standard 8⅝ ins. wide LNER variety. As grey continued, No.597 did not get either LNER or E suffix to its number, still shown in 19ins. yellow paint. Apart from No.627 (*see* Introduction), ex works 11th August 1923, Stratford used little or no black paint on the J15 until the engine got its 1924 number.

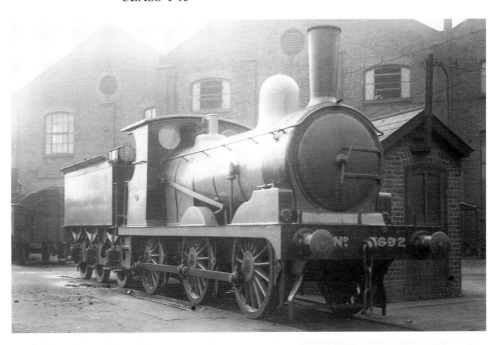

Stratford continued the use of grey paint through the 1920's so that some J15's never carried LNER initials. No.7692 was like this when ex works 5th February 1927, and this was its final repair because it was withdrawn 20th April 1929, still in grey. No.7829 was in grey at Cromer in 1926. Stratford works, February 1927.

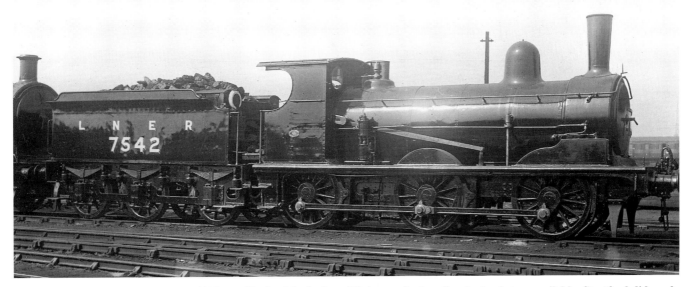

The official standard livery to June 1928 was black with single red lining, and when they had painters available, Stratford did apply it to some J15's. Livery changes were late in being made at Stratford. No.7542, with a coal guard on the tender, was ex works 26th March 1929. It could have been expected to be unlined and with number moved to cab, neither of which took place.

Ex works 9th May 1930, No.7850 was unlined and with the number moved to cab, but Stratford simply moved the LNER on the tender to a lower level and still used 7½ins letters. Stratford shed.

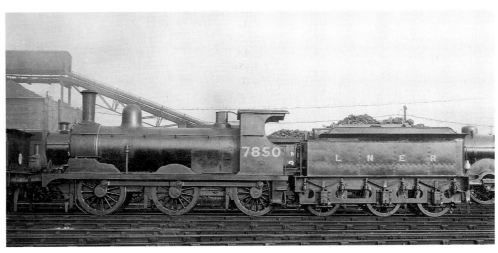

7520 cont./
King's Lynn 29/9/36.

RENUMBERED:
7520 25/3/25.
5437 10/11/46.

CONDEMNED: 18/9/50.
Cut up at Stratford.

_____

7521

Stratford.

To traffic 6/1899.

REPAIRS:
Str. 20/2—28/6/12.**G**.
Str. 5/10/17—15/2/18.**G**.
Str. 21/9—31/12/22.**G**.
Str. 26/8—6/12/27.**G**.
Coal guard on tender.
Str. 19/9—10/10/29.**G**.
Str. 2—19/12/31.**G**.
Str. 29/5—18/6/35.**G**.

BOILERS:
521.
521 28/6/12.
944 15/2/18.
925 31/12/22.
543 6/12/27.
2750 10/10/29.
2768 19/12/31.
2526 18/6/35.

SHEDS:
March.
Ipswich 21/6/28.
March 12/10/28.
Cambridge 25/9/32.

RENUMBERED:
7521 ?/?

CONDEMNED: 2/6/39.

_____

7522

Stratford.

To traffic 9/1899.

REPAIRS:
Str. ?/9—?/12/00.**G**.
After boiler explosion at
Westerfield.
Str. 17/3—28/5/15.**G**.
Str. 25/1—13/4/23.**G**.
Str. 20/9—27/12/24.**G**.
Str. ?/?—?/7/27.**G**.
Coal guard on tender.
Str. ?/?—?/9/29.**G**.

Str. 21/10—6/11/31.**G**.
Str. 20/12/33—8/1/34.**G**.

BOILERS:
522.
522 ?/12/00.
2509 28/5/15.
2508 13/4/23.
2532 27/12/24.
2555 ?/9/29.
2558 6/11/31.
2556 8/1/34.

SHED:
March.

RENUMBERED:
7522 27/12/24.

CONDEMNED: 13/3/36.

_____

7523

Stratford.

To traffic 9/1899.

REPAIRS:
Str. ?/?—?/6/09.**G**.
Str. 19/4—26/9/22.**G**.
Str. 28/7—1/12/24.**G**.
Str. 10/6—15/9/27.**G**.
Coal guard on tender.
Str. 16/10—16/11/29.**G**.
Str. 5/12/31—8/1/32.**G**.
Str. 26/5—9/7/34.**G**.
Str. 10—20/7/34.**L**.
Cab altered. Vacuum brake and
steam heat fitted.
Str. 31/12/35—10/2/36.**G**.
Str. 1—20/5/38.**G**.
Str. 22/4—17/5/40.**G**.
Str. 2/7—4/8/42.**G**.
Str. 13/5—2/6/45.**G**.
Str. 3/8—8/9/47.**G**.
Str. 15/6—1/7/49.**C/L**.
Str. 14—26/11/49.**G**.
Str. 8—30/5/51.**L/I**.
Str. 1/3—2/4/52.**G**.
Str. 14—29/9/53.**N/C**.
Str. 21/6—7/8/54.**C/L**.
Str. 13/9—30/10/54.**C/L**.
Str. 3—30/9/55.**G**.
Str. 11/6/58. *Not repaired.*

BOILERS:
523.
523 ?/6/09.
2564 16/11/29.
2769 8/1/32.
2778 20/5/38.
3318 17/5/40.
2778 4/8/42.
3368 2/6/45.

3337 8/9/47.
2575 26/11/49.
2575 reno. 23521 30/5/51.
23546 2/4/52.
23537 30/9/55.

SHEDS:
Lincoln.
March 3/3/25.
Cambridge 28/12/27.
Colchester 20/7/34.
Stratford 10/3/40.
Colchester 17/3/40.
Cambridge 6/5/46.
Bury St Edmunds 10/8/52.
Cambridge 19/10/52.

RENUMBERED:
7523 1/12/24.
5438 27/10/46.
65438 1/7/49.

CONDEMNED: 16/6/58.
Cut up at Stratford.

_____

7524

Stratford.

To traffic 10/1899.

REPAIRS:
Str. 10/3—23/6/14.**G**.
Str. 23/3—4/10/22.**G**.
Str. 28/9—15/12/25.**G**.
Str. 28/1—5/4/28.**G**.
Coal guard on tender.
Str. 17/3—10/4/30.**G**.
Str. 16/8—2/9/32.**G**.

BOILERS:
524.
2502 23/6/14.
938 4/10/22.
2505 15/12/25.
2566 5/4/28.
2574 10/4/30.
2788 2/9/32.

SHEDS:
March *at* 31/12/21.
Cambridge *by* 1924.
Stratford 23/6/26.
March 20/10/26.
Peterborough East 10/10/28.
March 18/3/29.
Cambridge 20/10/33.

RENUMBERED:
7524 15/12/25.

CONDEMNED: 13/3/36.

_____

7525

Stratford.

To traffic 10/1899.

REPAIRS:
Str. 14/10/13—15/1/14.**G**.
Str. 20/7—13/12/18.**G**.
Str. 15/2—6/9/22.**G**.
Str. 9/5—10/9/25.**G**.
Str. 16/11/27—10/2/28.**G**.
Coal guard on tender.
Str. 3—18/7/30.**G**.
Str. 14—30/12/32.**G**.

BOILERS:
525.
525 15/1/14.
2535 13/12/18.
2525 6/9/22.
2561 10/9/25.
645 10/2/28.
2568 18/7/30.
2539 30/12/32.

SHED:
Ipswich.

RENUMBERED:
7525 10/9/25.

CONDEMNED: 17/10/35.

_____

7526

Stratford.

To traffic 10/1899.

REPAIRS:
Str. 16/5—3/10/13.**G**.
Str. 10/2—13/6/23.**G**.
Str. 7/9—11/12/25.**G**.
Str. 20/12/27—20/4/28.**G**.
Coal guard on tender.
Str. 29/8—10/10/30.**G**.
Str. 31/10—23/11/33.**G**.
Str. 12/7—20/8/36.**G**.
Str. 29/9—12/11/40.**G**.
Str. 23/4—25/5/44.**G**.
Str. 3—10/9/45.**L**.
Str. 12/5—20/6/47.**G**.
Str. 16/9/51. *Not repaired.*

BOILERS:
526.
526 3/10/13.
2530 10/10/30.
2570 23/11/33.
2776 20/8/36.
2785 12/11/40.
2565 25/5/44.
3359 20/6/47.

7526 cont./
SHEDS:
Cambridge.
King's Lynn 16/5/28.
March 10/7/33.

RENUMBERED:
7526 11/12/25.
5439 22/12/46.

CONDEMNED: 19/11/51.
Cut up at Stratford.

_____

7640

Stratford.

To traffic 7/1899.

REPAIRS:
Str. 8/11/11—13/2/12.**G**.
Str. 4/11/15—28/3/16.**G**.
Str. 8/3—3/6/22.**G**.
Str. 2/1—27/2/25.**G**.
Str. 11/11/26—9/3/27.**G**.
Coal guard on tender.
Str. 8/6—26/7/29.**G**.
Str. 10/10—27/11/31.**G**.
Str. 26/5—6/7/34.**G**.
Str. 23/10—14/11/36.**G**.
Str. 12/2—24/3/39.**G**.
Str. 29/3—14/4/39.**L**.
Str. 17/8—15/9/41.**G**.
Str. 19/5—30/6/44.**G**.
Str. 28/7—30/8/46.**G**.
Str. 13—17/2/48.**N/C**.
Trip cock gear fitted.
Str. 13—27/8/49.**G**.
Str. 11/9—17/10/52.**G**.
Str. 12/7—24/8/56.**G**.
Str. 6/10/60. *Not repaired.*

BOILERS:
640.
640 13/2/12.
2516 28/3/16.
643 3/6/22.
569 26/7/29.
2532 27/11/31.
2716 6/7/34.
2766 14/11/36.
2745 24/3/39.
2563 15/9/41.
3353 30/6/44.
2764 30/8/46.
3339 27/8/49.
23564 17/10/52.
23551 24/8/56.

SHEDS:
Stratford.
Cambridge 11/6/27.
Norwich 3/10/27.
Stratford 14/12/27.

Southend 29/3/30.
Stratford 5/4/30.
Southend 19/4/30.
Stratford 3/5/30.
Colchester 25/9/39.
Stratford 3/12/39.
Colchester 28/12/40.
Stratford 13/4/41.
Colchester 19/1/46.
Stratford 25/2/48.
Colchester 22/10/50.
Stratford 12/11/50.
Colchester 4/3/51.
Stratford 8/7/51.

RENUMBERED:
7640 27/2/25.
5440 27/10/46.
65440 27/8/49.

CONDEMNED: 10/10/60.
Cut up at Stratford.

_____

7641

Stratford.

To traffic 7/1899.

REPAIRS:
Str. 19/7—10/10/11.**G**.
Str. 25/6—17/9/20.**G**.
Str. 12/9—8/12/22.**G**.
Str. 11/4—29/7/24.**G**.
Str. 3/9/26—5/2/27.**G**.
Str. 20/12/28—28/2/29.**G**.
Coal guard on tender.
Str. 19/1—27/2/31.**G**.
Str. 2—19/5/33.**G**.
Str. 17/1—8/2/35.**G**.
Str. 17/8—17/9/37.**G**.
Str. 27/8—11/10/40.**G**.
Trip cock gear fitted.
Str. 5/8—8/9/43.**N/C**.
Str. 23/2—17/3/44.**G**.
Str. 24/7—2/8/44.**L**.
Str. 26/5—25/6/46.**G**.
Str. 19—22/3/47.**N/C**.
Trip cock gear re-fitted.
Str. 4—21/10/49.**G**.
Str. 9/6—25/7/52.**G**.
Str. 15/8—16/9/55.**G**.

BOILERS:
641.
641 10/10/11.
520 17/9/20.
646 29/7/24.
551 5/2/27.
548 28/2/29.
2505 27/2/31.
2507 19/5/33.
2535 8/2/35.
3320 17/9/37.

2724 11/10/40.
2749 17/3/44.
2793 25/6/46.
2759 21/10/49.
23557 25/7/52.
23563 16/9/55.

SHEDS:
Ipswich.
Stratford 20/10/40.
Colchester 25/6/50.

RENUMBERED:
7641 29/7/24.
5441 2/12/46.
65441 21/10/49.

CONDEMNED: 8/10/58.
Cut up at Stratford.

_____

7642

Stratford.

To traffic 7/1899.

REPAIRS:
Str. 12/12/11—25/4/12.**G**.
Str. 13/9—16/12/22.**G**.
Str. 3/3—20/6/25.**G**.
Str. 15/7—1/10/27.**G**.
Coal guard on tender.
Str. 5/10—16/11/29.**G**.
Str. 4—28/1/32.**G**.
Str. 1—28/4/33.**L**.
Str. 4/12/34—4/1/35.**G**.
Str. 6/1—16/2/37.**G**.
Str. 16/8—25/9/39.**G**.
Str. 15/3—10/4/42.**L**.
Str. 10/10—13/11/43.**G**.
Str. 25/3—14/4/44.**N/C**.
Str. 24/1—18/3/46.**G**.
Str. 29/3—23/4/49.**G**.
Str. 16/2—8/3/52.**G**.
Str. 2—22/1/55.**G**.

BOILERS:
642.
642 25/4/12.
2516 16/12/22.
2511 1/10/27.
2512 16/11/29.
2535 28/1/32.
2772 4/1/35.
2787 16/2/37.
2780 25/9/39.
2745 13/11/43.
3312 18/3/46.
3301 23/4/49.
23543 8/3/52.
23587 22/1/55.

SHEDS:
Colchester.

Cambridge 22/2/33.
Bury St Edmunds 5/5/40.
Cambridge 10/8/52.

RENUMBERED:
7642 20/6/25.
5442 1/12/46.
65442 23/4/49.

CONDEMNED: 19/5/58.
Cut up at Stratford.

_____

7643

Stratford.

To traffic 7/1899.

REPAIRS:
Str. ?/?—?/12/10.**G**.
Str. 5/7—2/12/18.**G**.
Str. 4/12/22—7/2/23.**G**.
Str. 9/10/25—12/1/26.**G**.
Str. 28/4—15/8/28.**G**.
Coal guard on tender.
Str. 14/2—27/3/31.**G**.
Str. 20/8—22/9/33.**G**.
Str. 2/4—1/5/36.**G**.
Str. 28/10—25/11/38.**G**.
Str. 28/3—12/4/40.**G**.
Str. 22/6—26/7/41.**G**.
Str. 1/12/43—8/1/44.**G**.
Str. 27/2—30/3/46.**G**.
Str. 14—18/12/47.**L**.
Tender only.
Str. 1—6/2/48.**N/C**.
Trip cock gear fitted.
Str. 20/7—20/8/49.**G**.
Str. 17/11—2/12/50.**C/H**.
Str. 21/4—17/5/52.**G**.
Str. 29/11—31/12/55.**G**.

BOILERS:
643.
643 ?/12/10.
571 2/12/18.
517 12/1/26.
2552 15/8/28.
2547 27/3/31.
2744 22/9/33.
2533 1/5/36.
3312 25/11/38.
2752 12/4/40.
2767 26/7/41.
2780 8/1/44.
2758 30/3/46.
3351 20/8/49.
23505 2/12/50.
23553 17/5/52.
23529 31/12/55.

SHEDS:
Stratford.
March 1/6/29.

7643 cont./
Stratford 8/8/29.
Colchester 20/7/41.
Stratford 11/7/42.
Colchester 5/12/42.
Stratford 19/1/46.
Colchester 8/6/46.
Stratford 26/10/52.
Colchester 14/9/58.

RENUMBERED:
 7643 12/1/26.
 5443 17/11/46.
65443 20/8/49.

CONDEMNED: 7/12/59.
Cut up at Stratford.

7644

Stratford.

To traffic 7/1899.

REPAIRS:
Str. 18/7—17/10/11.**G.**
Str. 21/7—25/10/23.**G.**
Str. 4/6—15/10/26.**G.**
Str. 7/4—7/7/28.**G.**
Coal guard on tender.
Str. 12/4—30/5/30.**G.**
Str. 11/6—13/7/32.**G.**
Str. 29/1—20/2/35.**G.**
Str. 28/2—17/4/37.**G.**
Str. 10/3—20/5/39.**H.**
Str. 28/12/39—27/1/40.**G.**
Trip cock gear fitted.
Str. 24/12/42—13/2/43.**G.**
Str. 31/10—24/11/44.**G.**
Str. 25—27/3/47.**N/C.**
Trip cock gear re-fitted.
Str. 27/5—4/8/47.**G.**
Str. 28/1—17/2/51.**G.**
Str. 27/2—20/3/53.**N/C.**
Str. 23/8—18/9/54.**G.**

BOILERS:
 644.
 644 17/10/11.
 544 25/10/23.
 571 15/10/26.
2545 30/5/30.
2789 13/7/32.
3326 20/2/35.
2540 17/4/37.
3315 20/5/39.
2792 13/2/43.
3362 24/11/44.
2717 4/8/47.
23511 17/2/51.
23533 18/9/54.

SHEDS:
Stratford.

Norwich 3/10/25.
Stratford 16/12/25.
Parkeston 9/6/45.
Stratford 20/10/45.
Colchester 4/6/50.
Stratford 1/10/50.
Colchester 17/6/51.
Stratford 10/7/51.

RENUMBERED:
 7644 15/10/26.
 5444 1/9/46.
65444 17/2/51.

CONDEMNED: 20/10/58.
Cut up at Stratford.

7645

Stratford.

To traffic 8/1899.

REPAIRS:
Str. 18/12/10—18/1/13.**G.**
Str. 5/1—18/5/17.**G.**
Str. 14/8—21/10/22.**G.**
Str. 29/7—31/10/24.**G.**
Str. 1/4—22/7/27.**G.**
Str. 7/5—4/7/30.**G.**
Coal guard on tender.
Vacuum brake added 22/9/31.
Str. 12/11—16/12/32.**G.**
Str. 2—29/10/34.**G.**
Str. 4/3—12/4/37.**G.**
Str. 25/6—17/8/39.**G.**
Str. 26/10—22/11/41.**G.**
Str. 3—30/9/44.**G.**
Str. 30/3—6/5/47.**G.**
Str. 4—30/4/49.**G.**
Str. 22/10—10/11/51.**G.**
Str. 28/6—21/8/54.**G.**
Str. 10—25/8/55.**C/L.**
Str. 3—22/3/58.**G.**

BOILERS:
 645.
 645 18/1/13.
 921 18/5/17.
2527 31/10/24.
 571 4/7/30.
2566 16/12/32.
2540 29/10/34.
3317 12/4/37.
2570 17/8/39.
3311 22/11/41.
2774 30/9/44.
3339 6/5/47.
3329 30/4/49.
23533 10/11/51.
23531 21/8/54.
23509 22/3/58.

SHEDS:
Stratford.
Ipswich 21/10/27.
Colchester 11/1/31.
Stratford 25/9/39.
Colchester 3/12/39.
Stratford 6/6/42.
Colchester 5/12/42.
Parkeston 1/11/59.
Stratford 1/1/61.

RENUMBERED:
 7645 31/10/24.
 5445 8/12/46.
65445 30/4/49.

CONDEMNED: 1/8/62.
Cut up at Stratford.

7646

Stratford.

To traffic 8/1899.

REPAIRS:
Str. 11/3—4/8/10.**G.**
Str. 9/11/20—21/1/21.**G.**
Str. 1/10/23—12/1/24.**G.**
Str. 24/2—4/6/26.**G.**
Coal guard on tender.
Str. 14/12/28—8/2/29.**G.**
Str. 8/8—12/9/31.**G.**
Str. 11—22/1/32.**L.**
Vacuum brake added.
Str. 22/1—9/2/34.**G.**
Str. 29/5—24/6/36.**G.**
Str. 14/9—26/10/38.**G.**
Str. 25/1—21/2/41.**G.**
Trip cock gear fitted.
Str. 19/8—8/9/44.**G.**
Str. 24/11—21/12/46.**G.**
Str. 27—29/3/47.**N/C.**
Trip cock gear re-fitted.
Str. 25/9—8/10/49.**G.**
Str. 28/5—2/6/51.**N/C.**
Str. 30/6—21/8/52.**G.**
Str. 9/8—14/9/56.**G.**
Str. 12/12/60. *Not repaired.*

BOILERS:
 646.
 646 4/8/10.
2548 21/1/21.
 642 4/6/26.
2518 8/2/29.
2533 12/9/31.
2580 9/2/34.
3312 24/6/36.
2783 26/10/38.
2743 21/2/41.
2569 8/9/44.
3304 21/12/46.
3322 8/10/49.

23560 21/8/52.
23553 14/9/56.

SHEDS:
Cambridge .
Stratford 17/5/24.
Colchester 24/1/32.
Stratford 20/7/41.
Colchester 4/12/49.
Stratford 1/10/50.
Parkeston 25/2/51.
Stratford 8/7/51.
Colchester 14/12/58.
Stratford 6/12/59.

RENUMBERED:
 7646 4/6/26.
 5446 23/11/46.
65446 8/10/49.

CONDEMNED: 19/12/60.
Cut up at Stratford.

7647

Stratford.

To traffic 8/1899.

REPAIRS:
Str. 2/9—23/11/10.**G.**
Str. 31/8—19/11/20.**G.**
Str. 28/11/22—1/2/23.**G.**
Str. 16/5—9/9/25.**G.**
Str. 19/5—17/8/28.**G.**
Coal guard on tender.
Str. 2/5—15/6/31.**G.**
Str. 30/1—11/2/32.**L.**
Vacuum brake added.
Str. 4/3—11/4/34.**G.**
Str. 15/11—15/12/36.**G.**
Str. 17/6—22/7/39.**G.**
Str. 2/11—11/12/42.**G.**
Str. 15/4—5/5/45.**G.**
Str. 24/6—18/8/47.**H.**
Str. 7/6—3/7/48.**G.**
Str. 13/3—7/4/51.**G.**
Str. 8/11—4/12/54.**G.**

BOILERS:
 647.
 647 23/11/10.
 517 19/11/20.
 640 9/9/25.
2506 15/6/31.
2558 11/4/34.
3308 15/12/36.
2744 22/7/39.
3337 11/12/42.
3338 5/5/45.
3310 18/8/47.
23516 7/4/51.
23515 4/12/54.

For the cab numbers 12ins figures were normal but in 1930, when the two on the Duplicate List Nos.07038 and 07039 were to be done, the five figure numbers were put on in 9ins transfers. Neither engine ever got 12ins LNER.

Through to the end of the class in 1962, all had unlined black and by August 1930 Stratford had changed to 12ins tall LNER (*see* page 19, 3rd from top). Norwich, 24th October 1936.

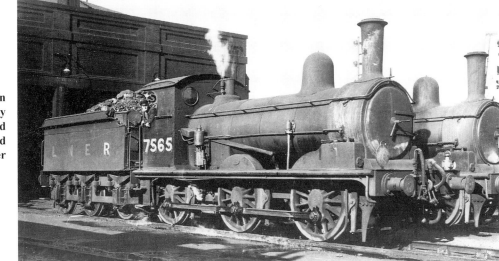

From July 1942 only NE was used on the tender and some never had LNER restored. No.7825 was ex works 14th July 1945 with NE and on Sunday 10th November 1946, at Lowestoft shed, it was renumbered 5352. Its next visit to works was for withdrawal on 29th May 1948.

Early in 1946 there was reversion to LNER, still in shaded transfers, so long as stocks lasted. No.5454 got them as late as 24th November 1947, ex works.

Ex works 8th September 1947, No.5438 had yellow painted and unshaded characters in Gill sans style, which had been chosen to replace the expensive transfers. Probably its change ten weeks earlier than No.5454 was due to the shortage of the figure 8 as so many of these were used in the 1924-45 period on Stratford maintained locomotives. Stratford works.

7647 cont./
SHEDS:
Stratford.
Ipswich 31/10/40.

RENUMBERED:
7647 9/9/25.
5447 18/8/46.
65447 3/7/48.

CONDEMNED: 13/4/59.
Cut up at Stratford.

7648

Stratford.

To traffic 9/1899.

REPAIRS:
Str. 28/7—15/10/15.**G.**
Str. 26/11/20—5/3/21.**G.**
Str. 27/11/23—19/2/24.**G.**
Str. 2/9—26/11/26.**G.**
Str. 26/11/28—1/2/29.**G.**
Coal guard on tender.
Str. 10/10—20/11/31.**G.**
Vacuum brake added.
Str. 12/7—24/8/34.**G.**
Str. 4/3—10/4/37.**G.**
Str. 20/8—3/10/39.**G.**
Str. 21/2—2/4/43.**G.**
Str. 19/8—7/9/45.**G.**
Str. 17/8—13/9/48.**G.**
Str. 10—24/6/49.**C/L.**
Str. 8/2—3/3/51.**G.**
Str. 10—27/11/52.**N/C.**
Str. 7/12/53—2/1/54.**G.**
Str. 13/1—8/2/57.**G.**

BOILERS:
648.
2512 15/10/15.
646 5/3/21.
2558 19/2/24.
2535 1/2/29.
2531 20/11/31.
2793 24/8/34.
2544 10/4/37.
3308 3/10/39.
2558 2/4/43.
3333 7/9/45.
2784 13/9/48.
23514 3/3/51.
23584 2/1/54.
23549 8/2/57.

SHEDS:
Stratford.
Cambridge 10/7/40.
Kings Lynn 26/10/41.
Cambridge 1/2/42.
Stratford 2/5/47.
Colchester 10/5/47.

Stratford 6/12/59.

RENUMBERED:
Still **648** *at* 19/2/24.
7648 26/11/26.
5448 13/10/46.
65448 11/9/48.

CONDEMNED: 7/3/60.
Cut up at Stratford.

7649

Stratford.

To traffic 9/1899.

REPAIRS:
Str. 2/3—18/6/17.**G.**
Str. 13/6—28/10/19.**G.**
Str. 5/8—27/10/21.**G.**
Str. 23/8—22/12/23.**G.**
Str. 30/10—24/12/25.**G.**
Str. 7/7—28/9/28.**G.**
Coal guard on tender.
Str. 30/8—10/10/30.**G.**
Str. 22—26/2/32.**L.**
Vacuum brake added.
Str. 20/3—12/4/33.**G.**
Str. 22/10—13/11/35.**G.**
Str. 18/6—15/8/38.**G.**
Str. 23/3—16/4/41.**G.**
Str. 20/2—18/3/44.**G.**
Str. 2—20/12/45.**G.**
Str. 23/11—21/12/46.**L.**
Str. 1—6/2/48.**N/C.**
Trip cock gear fitted.
Str. 29/8—3/10/48.**G.**
Str. 8—27/10/51.**G.**
Str. 5/12/55—7/1/56.**G.**

BOILERS:
649.
904 18/6/17.
643 28/10/19.
647 27/10/21.
2550 28/9/28.
2567 10/10/30.
485 12/4/33.
2543 13/11/35.
3305 15/8/38.
2728 16/4/41.
2767 18/3/44.
2577 20/12/45.
3315 3/10/48.
23532 27/10/51.
23577 7/1/56.

SHEDS:
Stratford.
Colchester 25/9/39.
Stratford 3/12/39.
Colchester 20/7/41.
Stratford 6/6/42.

Colchester 5/12/42.
Stratford 19/1/46.

RENUMBERED:
7649 24/12/25.
5449 15/9/46.
65449 2/10/48.

CONDEMNED: 14/12/59.
Cut up at Stratford.

7552

Stratford.

To traffic 5/1906.

REPAIRS:
Str. 25/1—31/5/18.**G.**
Str. 19/12/19—18/3/20.**G.**
Str. 6/11/22—13/1/23.**G.**
Str. 8/5—17/9/25.**G.**
Str. 12/5—1/8/28.**G.**
Coal guard on tender.
Str. 17/2—9/4/31.**G.**
Str. 21/12/33—22/1/34.**G.**
Str. 17/2—6/4/37.**G.**
Str. 11/10—24/11/39.**G.**
Trip cock gear fitted.
Str. 20/3—30/4/43.**G.**
Str. 20/8—21/9/44.**G.**
Str. 4—17/11/45.**G.**
Str. 8/7—2/8/46.**L.**
Str. 25—28/3/47.**N/C.**
Trip cock gear re-fitted.
Str. 21/4—14/5/49.**G.**
Str. 5/6—1/7/52.**G.**
Str. 8/12/53—15/1/54.**C/L.**
Str. 7/1—6/4/55.**C/H.**
Str. 26/2—5/4/57.**L/I.**

BOILERS:
552.
551 31/5/18.
568 18/3/20.
2562 17/9/25.
2580 9/4/31.
565 22/1/34.
3326 6/4/37.
2577 24/11/39.
3302 30/4/43.
2570 21/9/44.
3303 17/11/45.
3305 14/5/49.
23505 1/7/52.
23536 6/4/55.

SHEDS:
Stratford.
Cambridge 25/6/26.
Stratford 17/11/26.
Cambridge 5/1/29.
King's Lynn 9/5/29.
Colchester 25/5/39.

Stratford 8/9/40.
Cambridge 26/10/58.

RENUMBERED:
7552 17/9/25.
5450 3/1/47.
65450 14/5/49.

CONDEMNED: 26/10/61.
To Doncaster for c/u 26/10/61.

7553

Stratford.

To traffic 5/1906.

REPAIRS:
Str. 18/2—5/6/17.**G.**
Str. 10/10—24/12/19.**G.**
Str. 7/12/22—10/2/23.**G.**
Str. 14/11/24—10/2/25.**G.**
Str. 18/8—17/11/27.**G.**
Coal guard on tender.
Str. 3/4—30/5/30.**G.**
Str. 26/10—18/11/32.**G.**
Str. 23/3—9/5/35.**G.**
Str. 18/9—16/10/37.**G.**
Str. 19/4—19/5/41.**G.**
Str. 19/9—20/1/44.**G.**
Str. 2—30/3/46.**G.**
Str. 8/5—12/6/48.**G.**
Str. 22/4—12/5/51.**G.**
Str. 8—26/9/53.**G.**
Str. 6/1—8/2/57.**G.**
Str. 23/9/59. *Not repaired.*

BOILERS:
553.
557 5/6/17.
2540 24/12/19.
2553 10/2/25.
485 30/5/30.
2526 18/11/32.
2789 9/5/35.
3327 16/10/37.
2749 19/5/41.
2754 20/1/44.
3347 30/3/46.
3330 12/6/48.
23520 12/5/51.
23583 26/9/53.
23532 8/2/57.

SHEDS:
Stratford.
Cambridge 2/1/29.

RENUMBERED:
7553 10/2/25.
5451 13/10/46.
65451 12/6/48.

7553 cont./
CONDEMNED: 28/9/59.
Cut up at Stratford.

_____

7554

Stratford.

To traffic 6/1906.

REPAIRS:
Str. 28/3—14/9/17.**G.**
Str.(shed) ?/?—7/11/17.**G.**
Str. ?/?—?/?/20.**G.**
Str. 16/1—10/3/23.**G.**
Str. 16/5—17/9/25.**G.**
Str. 10/2—15/5/28.**G.**
Coal guard on tender.
Str. 26/7—5/9/30.**G.**
Str. 11/7—16/8/32.**G.**
Str. 17/5—23/6/34.**G.**
Str. 8/3—7/4/36.**G.**
Str. 29/5—18/6/38.**G.**
Str. 17/6—19/7/39.**H.**
Str. 19/12/40—22/1/41.**G.**
Trip cock gear fitted.
Str. 22/6—3/9/43.**G.**
Str. 18/11—1/12/45.**G.**
Str. 19—22/3/47.**N/C.**
Trip cock gear re-fitted.
Str. 3/2—20/3/48.**G.**
Str. 12—21/5/49.**C/L.**
Str. 3/8—1/9/51.**G.**
Str. 24/10—18/11/55.**G.**

BOILERS:
554.
520 14/9/17.
554 7/11/17.
542 ?/?/20.
2567 15/5/28.
2553 5/9/30.
2673 16/8/32.
2724 23/6/34.
3305 7/4/36.
2772 18/6/38.
3301 19/7/39.
2765 22/1/41.
2720 3/9/43.
2786 1/12/45.
3346 20/3/48.
23527 1/9/51.
23522 18/11/55.

SHEDS:
Stratford.
March 31/5/29.
Stratford 23/9/29.
Southend 28/6/30.
Stratford 5/7/30.
Colchester 8/9/40.
Stratford 20/7/41.

RENUMBERED:
7554 17/9/25.
5452 2/1/47.
E5452 20/3/48.
65452 21/5/49.

CONDEMNED: 7/12/59.
Cut up at Stratford.

_____

7555

Stratford.

To traffic 6/1906.

REPAIRS:
Str. ?/?—?/6/20.**G.**
Str. 27/7—22/12/23.**G.**
Str. 6/11—31/12/25.**G.**
Str. 31/8—16/10/28.**G.**
Coal guard on tender.
Str. 16/1—14/2/30.**G.**
Str. 29/3—25/6/30.**L.**
For attention to brake.
Str. 14/3—1/5/31.**G.**
Str. 6/7—1/8/33.**G.**
Str. 20/1—14/2/36.**G.**
Str. 4—30/8/38.**G.**
Str. 26/12/40—1/1/41.**L.**
Str. 4—29/3/41.**G.**
Str. 12/9—15/10/43.**G.**
Str. 13/1—2/2/46.**G.**
Str. 25/2—1/3/48.**N/C.**
Trip cock gear fitted.
Str. 28/8—16/9/49.**G.**
Str. 26/9—5/10/49.**N/C.**
Str. 13—25/4/53.**G.**
Str. 18/7—23/8/57.**G.**
Str. 20/1—17/2/61.**N/C.**

BOILERS:
555.
2518 ?/6/20.
2570 16/10/28.
2744 1/5/31.
545 1/8/33.
3306 14/2/36.
3309 30/8/38.
2746 29/3/41.
2766 15/10/43.
2787 2/2/46.
3312 16/9/49.
23576 25/4/53.
23502 23/8/57.

SHEDS:
Cambridge .
Stratford 17/5/24.
Cambridge 24/6/26.
Norwich 2/10/26.
Stratford 21/12/26.
Cambridge 11/6/27.
Stratford 6/10/27.
Southend 28/12/29.

Stratford 4/1/30.
Southend 22/2/30.
Stratford 15/3/30.
Southend 1/11/30.
Stratford 15/11/30.
Colchester 25/9/39.
Stratford 3/12/39.
Colchester 8/9/40.
Stratford 19/1/46.
Parkeston 10/5/47.
Stratford 25/2/48.
Parkeston 8/7/51.
Stratford 1/1/61.

RENUMBERED:
7555 31/12/25
5453 16/6/46.
65453 16/9/49.

CONDEMNED: 6/8/62.
*Sold for scrap to J.Cashmore,
Great Bridge, 11/62.*

_____

7556

Stratford.

To traffic 6/1906.

REPAIRS:
Str. 16/5—24/10/17.**G.**
Str. 10/10/19—23/1/20.**G.**
Str. 20/11/22—24/2/23.**G.**
Str. 19/3—8/7/25.**G.**
Str. 7/7—27/9/27.**G.**
Coal guard on tender.
Str. 4/4—9/5/30.**G.**
Str. 6—30/9/32.**G.**
Str. 21/12/34—22/1/35.**G.**
Str. 9/12/36—23/1/37.**G.**
Str. 4/3—20/4/40.**G.**
Trip cock gear fitted.
Str. 26/12/42—19/2/43.**G.**
Str. 22/4—5/5/45.**G.**
Str. 19—21/3/47.**N/C.**
Trip cock gear re-fitted.
Str. 11/9—24/11/47.**G.**
Str. 11—31/3/51.**G.**
Str. 5—30/10/54.**G.**
Str. 6/11—7/12/57.**C/H.**

BOILERS:
556.
553 24/10/17.
2543 23/1/20.
2560 27/9/27.
2507 9/5/30.
2574 30/9/32.
2787 22/1/35.
2716 23/1/37.
2542 20/4/40.
3343 19/2/43.
2573 5/5/45.
3344 24/11/47.

23515 31/3/51.
23509 30/10/54.
23501 7/12/57.

SHEDS:
Stratford.
Cambridge 26/6/26.
Stratford 10/1/27.
Ipswich 21/10/27.
March 22/6/28.
Ipswich 16/10/28.
Stratford 24/4/40.
Colchester 9/11/41.
Stratford 10/5/47.
Colchester 2/7/50.
Stratford 1/10/50.
Ipswich 26/10/58.

RENUMBERED:
7556 8/7/25.
5454 15/6/46.
65454 31/3/51.

CONDEMNED: 22/5/59.
Cut up at Stratford.

_____

7557

Stratford.

To traffic 6/1906.

REPAIRS:
Str. 19/10/16—12/4/17.**G.**
Str. 11/6—22/9/23.**G.**
Str. 24/12/25—30/3/26.**G.**
Coal guard on tender.
Str. 31/8—31/10/28.**G.**
Str. 31/12/30—13/2/31.**G.**
Str. 16/5—13/6/33.**G.**
Str. 12/1—11/2/36.**G.**
Str. 3—21/10/37.**L.**
Str. 15/3—9/4/38.**G.**
Str. 4/9—31/10/40.**G**
Trip cock gear fitted.
Str. 18/10—19/11/42.**H.**
Str. 31/10—26/11/43.**G.**
Str. 17/2—18/3/46.**G.**
Str. 28—29/3/47.**N/C.**
Trip cock gear re-fitted.
Str. 18/5—11/6/49.**G.**
Str. 9—19/4/51.**C/H.**
Str. 6—29/10/52.**G.**
Str. 11/9—3/11/56.**G.**

BOILERS:
557.
569 12/4/17.
2547 22/9/23.
550 30/3/26.
438 31/10/28.
2503 13/2/31.
2554 13/6/33.
3311 11/2/36.

7557 cont./
2765 9/4/38.
3303 31/10/40.
3301 19/11/42.
2746 26/11/43.
2766 18/3/46.
3380 11/6/49.
23519 19/4/51.
23567 29/10/52.
23543 3/11/56.

SHEDS:
Stratford.
Cambridge 26/6/26.
Stratford 3/12/26.
Cambridge 11/6/27.
Stratford 28/9/27.
Southend 15/3/30.
Stratford 19/4/30.
Southend 26/4/30.
Stratford 10/5/30.
Colchester 6/6/42.
Stratford 5/12/42.

RENUMBERED:
7557 30/3/26.
5455 23/6/46.
65455 11/6/49.

CONDEMNED: 18/3/60.
Cut up at Stratford.

7558

Stratford.

To traffic 6/1906.

REPAIRS:
Str. 7/6—6/9/18.**G.**
Str. ?/?—?/7/20.**G.**
Str. 28/7—2/11/21.**G.**
Str. 5/7—15/10/24.**G.**
Str. 2/12/26—11/3/27.**G.**
Coal guard on tender.
Str. 14/6—26/7/29.**G.**
Str. 28/11/31—8/1/32.**G.**
Str. 21/4—15/6/34.**G.**
Str. 17/1—20/2/37.**G.**
Str. 4/6—11/7/39.**G.**
Str. 31/8—15/10/41.**G.**
Str. 13/8—23/10/43.**G.**
Str. 7—20/10/45.**G.**
Str. 10/3—22/4/48.**G.**
Str. 4—30/6/51.**G.**
Str. 25/1—20/2/54.**G.**
Str. 23/4—24/5/57.**G.**
Str. 2—27/9/57.**C/L.**

BOILERS:
558.
520 6/9/18.
555 ?/7/20.
553 2/11/21.

520 15/10/24.
646 11/3/27.
644 26/7/29.
2766 8/1/32.
2727 15/6/34.
2780 20/2/37.
2766 11/7/39.
2745 15/10/41.
2577 23/10/43.
3336 20/10/45.
3395 22/4/48.
23523 30/6/51.
23586 20/2/54.
23561 24/5/57.

SHEDS:
Stratford.
Cambridge 11/6/27.
Stratford 28/9/27.
Colchester 21/10/27.
Stratford 25/9/39.
Colchester 3/12/39.
Stratford 4/9/49.
Colchester 6/11/49.

RENUMBERED:
7558 15/10/24.
5456 6/10/46.
65456 17/4/48.

CONDEMNED: 8/9/58.
Cut up at Stratford.

7559

Stratford.

To traffic 6/1906.

REPAIRS:
Str. 12/4—18/6/18.**G.**
Str. 2/3—30/5/22.**G.**
Str. 13/9—13/12/24.**G.**
Str.10/6—30/9/27.**G.**
Coal guard on tender.
Str. 1/11—14/12/28.**H.**
Str. 19/4—26/6/30.**G.**
Str. 19/3—15/4/32.**G.**
Str. 16/10—5/11/34.**G.**
Str. 30/1—6/3/37.**H.**
Str. 8/5—3/6/38.**G.**
Str. 15/8—26/9/41.**G.**
Str. 1/4—5/5/44.**G.**
Str. 3/7—4/10/46.**G.**
Str. 17/1—24/2/49.**G.**
Str. 19/11—8/12/51.**G.**
Str. 6—24/12/54.**G.**
Str. 17/2—15/3/58.**G.**

BOILERS:
559.
919 18/6/18.
2517 30/5/22.
546 13/12/24.

2534 14/12/28.
2560 26/6/30.
2772 15/4/32.
2519 5/11/34.
2772 6/3/37.
3311 3/6/38.
2763 26/9/41.
2795 5/5/44.
3380 4/10/46.
2781 24/2/49.
23536 8/12/51.
23526 24/12/54.
23516 15/3/58.

SHEDS:
Ipswich.
March 24/2/33.
Cambridge 17/6/34.
March 16/10/34.
Cambridge 14/9/39.

RENUMBERED:
7559 13/12/24.
5457 1/10/46.
65457 19/2/49.

CONDEMNED: 11/2/62.

7560

Stratford.

To traffic 6/1906.

REPAIRS:
Str. 23/8—17/12/18.**G.**
Str. 6/12/23—23/2/24.**G.**
Str. 15/4—19/8/26.**G.**
Coal guard on tender.
Str. 26/1—11/4/29.**G.**
Str. 4/6—29/7/31.**G.**
Str. 21/11—8/12/33.**G.**
Str. 13/7—12/8/36.**G.**
Str. 12/8—21/9/38.**G.**
Str. 21/2—24/3/41.**G.**
Str. 25/7—18/9/43.**G.**
Str. 2/12/45—4/1/46.**G.**
Str. 7/4—12/5/49.**G.**
Str. 16/3—17/4/53.**G.**
Str. 2—17/3/56.**G.**
Str. 27/5—21/6/57.**G.**

BOILERS:
560.
2536 17/12/18.
2557 23/2/24.
2654 11/4/29.
2556 29/7/31.
3315 8/12/33.
2580 12/8/36.
2749 21/9/38.
2782 24/3/41.
3312 18/9/43.
2782 4/1/46.

2795 12/5/49.
23510 17/4/53.
23548 17/3/56.

SHEDS:
Stratford.
Norwich 3/10/25.
Stratford 16/12/25.
Cambridge 11/6/27.
Stratford 28/9/27.
March 19/6/28.
Stratford 12/10/28.
Southend 5/7/30.
Stratford 2/8/30.
Southend 9/8/30.
Stratford 1/11/30.
Colchester 20/7/41.
Stratford 19/1/46.
Parkeston 5/7/47.
March 13/3/60.

RENUMBERED:
Still **560** *at* 23/2/24.
7560 19/8/26.
5458 15/9/46.
65458 12/5/49.

CONDEMNED: 31/10/61.
Cut up at Stratford.

7561

Stratford.

To traffic 6/1906.

REPAIRS:
Str. 18/1—7/6/18.**G.**
Str. 27/4—14/7/23.**G.**
Str. 31/3—27/8/26.**G.**
Str. 19/1—22/3/29.**G.**
Coal guard on tender.
Str. 22/10—11/12/31.**G.**
Str. 19/10—26/11/35.**G.**
Str. 14/7—19/8/38.**G.**
Str. 22/10—18/11/41.**G.**
Str. 21—31/7/43.**G.**
Str. 26/3—27/4/44.**G.**
Str. 23/6—9/8/46.**G.**
Str. 17/5—18/6/49.**G.**
Str. 17/5—17/6/52.**G.**
Str. 25/12/55—10/2/56.**G.**

BOILERS:
561.
645 7/6/18.
565 27/8/26.
642 22/3/29.
2765 11/12/31.
2783 26/11/35.
2777 19/8/38.
2766 18/11/41.
3304 31/7/43.
2749 9/8/46.

7561 cont./
3379 18/6/49.
23555 17/6/52.
23527 10/2/56.

SHEDS:
Stratford.
Cambridge 11/6/27.
Stratford 28/9/27.
March 19/6/28.
Stratford 11/10/28.
Norwich 3/8/29.
Yarmouth 11/1/31.
Norwich 13/12/31.
Peterborough East 7/4/33.
Ipswich 6/7/36.
Stratford 29/11/59.

RENUMBERED:
7561 27/8/26.
5459 8/9/46.
65459 18/6/49.

CONDEMNED: 10/2/60.
Cut up at Stratford.

7562

Stratford.

To traffic 2/1912.

REPAIRS:
YEC. 16/12/19—26/11/20.**G.**
Nor. 22/12/22—2/3/23.**H.**
Nor. 24/9—6/12/24.**H.**
Str. 8/6—26/11/26.**G.**
Coal guard on tender.
Str. 13/5—21/6/29.**G.**
Str. 31/5—17/7/31.**G.**
Str. 8—28/2/34.**G.**
Str. 26/2—3/4/37.**G.**
Str. 31/8—24/10/39.**G.**
Str. 6/12/42—23/1/43.**G.**
Str. 29/9—18/10/43.**L.**
Str. 1/10—11/11/44.**G.**
Str. 23/9—26/10/45.**G.**
Str. 7/8—18/9/47.**G.**
Str. 12/7—6/8/49.**C/H.**
Str. 17/9—7/10/50.**G.**
Str. 17/5—18/6/53.**G.**
Str. 9/10—16/11/56.**C/L.**
Str. 18/3—14/4/58.**G.**

BOILERS:
562.
2538 26/11/26.
565 21/6/29.
2500 17/7/31.
3317 28/2/34.
2519 3/4/37.
2793 24/10/39.
3339 23/1/43.
3311 11/11/44.

3317 26/10/45.
3366 18/9/47.
3303 6/8/49.
23502 7/10/50.
23508 18/6/53.
23520 14/4/58.

SHEDS:
Norwich.
Lowestoft 27/7/35.
Norwich 23/5/37.
Lowestoft 26/9/37.
Norwich 4/4/39.
Ipswich 5/11/47.
Norwich 18/11/47.
Lowestoft 18/9/55.
Norwich 11/9/60.
Stratford 18/12/60.

RENUMBERED:
7562 6/12/24.
5460 2/9/46.
65460 6/8/49.

CONDEMNED: 5/9/62.
Sold for scrap to J.Cashmore, Great Bridge, 11/62.

7563

Stratford.

To traffic 2/1912.

REPAIRS:
Str. 7/6—24/9/21.**G.**
Pbo. 26/3—15/5/23.**H.**
Str. 20/1—21/3/25.**G.**
Str. 22/9—17/12/27.**G.**
Coal guard on tender.
Str. 19/3—9/5/30.**G.**
Str. 10/9—12/10/32.**G.**
Str. 3/9—10/10/35.**G.**
Str. 7/6—2/7/38.**G.**
Str. 6/7—16/8/41.**G.**
Str. 24—30/6/43.**L.**
Str. 6/10—13/11/43.**G.**
Str. 24/3—16/4/46.**G.**
Str. 8/9—19/10/48.**G.**
Str. 6/7—4/8/51.**G.**
Str. 18/10—13/11/54.**G.**
Str. 6/6—2/8/57.**G.**

BOILERS:
563.
641 24/9/21.
566 21/3/25.
507 17/12/27.
2526 9/5/30.
2543 12/10/32.
2777 10/10/35.
2563 2/7/38.
2752 16/8/41.
2689 13/11/43.

2768 16/4/46.
3371 19/10/48.
23526 4/8/51.
23502 13/11/54.
23574 2/8/57.

SHEDS:
Cambridge .
Peterborough East 22/10/31.
March 11/12/31.
Cambridge 15/12/40.
March 9/2/41.
South Lynn 1/3/43.
Cambridge 15/7/43.
Bury St Edmunds 24/11/46.
Cambridge 13/6/47.

RENUMBERED:
7563 21/3/25.
5461 1/12/46.
65461 16/10/48.

CONDEMNED: 28/4/60.
Cut up at Stratford.

7564

Stratford.

To traffic 3/1912.

REPAIRS:
Str. 9/3—13/5/20.**G.**
Str. 12/10—1/12/23.**G.**
Str. 4/8—8/12/26.**G.**
Str. 17/4—15/6/29.**G.**
Coal guard on tender.
Str. 27/2—19/3/32.**G.**
Str. 30/1—23/2/35.**G.**
Str. 9/8—2/9/37.**G.**
Str. 29/1—1/3/40.**G.**
Str. 18/7—19/9/43.**G.**
Str. 22/7—11/8/45.**G.**
Str. 24/5—4/7/47.**G.**
Str. 4/2—3/3/49.**L.**
Str. 12/3—5/4/50.**G.**
Str. 19/4—14/5/53.**G.**
Str. 11/5—14/6/57.**G.**

BOILERS:
564.
551 13/5/20.
644 8/12/26.
549 15/6/29.
2573 19/3/32.
3327 23/2/35.
2781 2/9/37.
2689 1/3/40.
2747 19/9/43.
3337 11/8/45.
2761 4/7/47.
2780 5/4/50.
23525 14/5/53.
23566 14/6/57.

SHEDS:
Norwich.
Yarmouth 23/9/28.
Norwich 30/9/28.
Lowestoft 4/10/31.
Norwich 25/10/31.
Yarmouth 25/10/33.
Lowestoft 26/5/34.
Norwich 23/1/35.
Yarmouth 3/9/39.
Norwich 8/10/39.
Yarmouth 24/11/40.
Norwich 4/3/45.
Yarmouth 29/4/45.
Lowestoft 7/9/45.
Norwich 16/3/47.
Lowestoft 12/10/47.
Norwich 26/6/60.
Stratford 8/1/61.

RENUMBERED:
7564 8/12/26.
5462 10/11/46.
65462 26/2/49.

WITHDRAWN: 16/9/62.
Sold to North Norfolk Railway for preservation.

7565

Stratford.

To traffic 3/1912.

REPAIRS:
Str. 13/9—20/12/18.**G.**
Str. 6/10/22—19/1/23.**G.**
Str. 2/12/24—26/2/25.**G.**
Str. 7/10/27—20/1/28.**G.**
Coal guard on tender.
Str. 19/8—10/10/30.**G.**
Str. 21/7—28/8/33.**G.**
Str. 11/12/35—17/1/36.**G.**
Str. 14/2—14/3/38.**G.**
Str. 17/7—24/8/40.**G.**
Trip cock gear fitted.
Str. 1/7—18/8/43.**G.**
Str. 11—29/9/45.**G.**
Str. 31/3—1/4/47.**N/C.**
Trip cock gear re-fitted.
Str. 21/3—21/4/48.**G.**
Str. 24/8—8/9/51.**G.**
Str. 15/8—10/9/55.**G.**

BOILERS:
565.
559 20/12/18.
566 19/1/23.
553 26/2/25.
2525 20/1/28.
2501 10/10/30.
3306 28/8/33.
2750 17/1/36.

Whilst the British Railways regional E prefix was being applied, it was put on four J15's in 1948: ᴇ5391 (16th March), ᴇ5452 (20th March), ᴇ5469 (25th January), and ᴇ5475 (11th February).

Beginning with No.65467 on 5th April 1948, the full BR number was used and with unshaded figures. No difficulty was found in putting five 12ins figures on the cab side. Note that the modified 6 (and 9) was used and that the tender letters were 10ins high. No.65431 was renumbered when ex works 27th April 1948, and this style was in use to August of that year. Colchester.

In August 1948 the 6 and 9 cab numbers were changed from the modified to a true Gill sans style and the numbers were made 10ins high to match tender letters. No.65465, ex works 25th August 1949, was probably the last J15 to have tender lettering. Because Stratford did not begin to fit smokebox number plates until late September 1948, their castings included the correct Gill sans numbers 6 and 9. Stratford, September 1951.

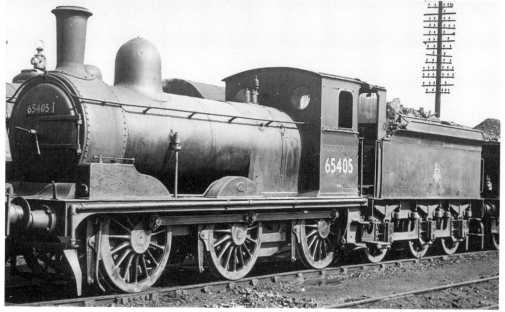

(left) From September 1949 the tender lettering changed to the British Railways emblem, only the 15$\frac{1}{2}$ins high version being used for J15 class.

(below) No.65464, ex works on 14th May 1957, had the BR crest instead of the emblem and sixteen were so treated: 65420, 65445, 65453, 65454, 65456, 65457, 65458, 65460, 65461, 65462, 65464, 65465, 65469, 65472, 65476 and 65478. Stratford works.

7565 cont./
2724 14/3/38.
3312 24/8/40.
2787 18/8/43.
2547 29/9/45.
3335 21/4/48.
23529 8/9/51.
23569 10/9/55.

SHEDS:
Norwich.
Stratford 20/1/28.
Norwich 20/4/28.
Yarmouth 3/8/30.
Norwich 11/1/31.
Lowestoft 5/4/31.
Norwich 9/9/33.
Yarmouth 31/3/37.
Norwich 3/10/37.
Stratford 29/8/40.
Colchester 11/7/42.
Stratford 5/12/42.
Colchester 19/1/46.
Stratford 10/5/47.

RENUMBERED:
7565 26/2/25.
5463 7/12/46.
65463 17/4/48.

CONDEMNED: 18/11/59.
Cut up at Stratford.

7566

Stratford.

To traffic 3/1912.

REPAIRS:
Str. 22/11/18—9/5/19.**G.**
Str. 25/1—15/6/22.**G.**
Str. 5/9—31/10/24.**G.**
Str. 10/8—23/9/25.**G.**
Str. 20/12/26—3/3/27.**G.**
Coal guard on tender.
Str. 15/3—8/5/29.**G.**
Str. 18/6—14/8/31.**G.**
Str. 30/10—17/11/33.**G.**
Str. 10/12/35—7/1/36.**G.**
Str. 27/9—20/10/37.**G.**
Str. 4/2—26/3/40.**G.**
Trip cock gear fitted.
Str. 15/11—12/12/42.**G.**
Str. 11—24/2/45.**G.**
Str. 24—29/3/47.**N/C.**
Trip cock gear re-fitted.
Str. 7/8—26/9/47.**G.**
Str. 18/5—3/6/50.**G.**
Str. 5—28/8/53.**G.**
Str. 26—30/1/54.**N/C.**
Str. 8/4—14/5/57.**G.**
Str. 14/5—5/6/58.**C/L.**
Str. 21/12/60—20/1/61.**N/C.**

BOILERS:
566.
565 9/5/19.
563 15/6/22.
549 3/3/27.
2558 8/5/29.
565 14/8/31.
3311 17/11/33.
2765 7/1/36.
2752 20/10/37.
2792 26/3/40.
3338 12/12/42.
2792 24/2/45.
3325 26/9/47.
3368 3/6/50.
23501 28/8/53.
23573 14/5/57.

SHEDS:
Ipswich.
Norwich 8/5/29.
Yarmouth 17/3/34.
Norwich 15/1/35.
Lowestoft 23/1/35.
Norwich 17/12/35.
Lowestoft 9/6/37.
Norwich 26/9/37.
Yarmouth 23/1/38.
Colchester 17/5/39.
Stratford 8/9/40.
Colchester 6/6/42.
Stratford 5/12/42.

RENUMBERED:
7566 31/10/24.
5464 2/1/47.
65464 3/6/50.

CONDEMNED: 16/9/62.

7567

Stratford.

To traffic 3/1912.

REPAIRS:
Str. 25/3—29/4/16.**G.**
Str. 4/2—26/5/21.**G.**
Str. 4/5—31/8/23.**G.**
Str. 15/9—27/11/25.**G.**
Str. 18/8—9/11/27.**G.**
Coal guard on tender.
Str. 3/4—16/5/30.**G.**
Str. 9/8—7/9/32.**G.**
Str. 23/10—7/12/34.**G.**
Str. 16/5—15/6/37.**G.**
Str. 9—14/12/37.**L.**
Str. 20/8—10/10/39.**G.**
Str. 27/3—22/5/43.**G.**
Str. 18/11—15/12/45.**G.**
Str. 11—25/8/49.**G.**
Str. 4—23/2/52.**G.**
Str. 17/12/53—20/1/54.**C/L.**

Str. 3/1—12/2/55.**G.**
Str. 11/10—2/11/57.**G.**
Str. 12—17/12/60.**N/C.**

BOILERS:
567.
2517 29/4/16.
544 26/5/21.
642 31/8/23.
543 27/11/25.
545 9/11/27.
2566 16/5/30.
2787 7/9/32.
2566 7/12/34.
2793 15/6/37.
3317 10/10/39.
2783 22/5/43.
2571 15/12/45.
3345 25/8/49.
23544 23/2/52.
23516 12/2/55.
23576 2/11/57.

SHEDS:
Colchester.
Stratford 25/9/39.
Colchester 3/12/39.
Ipswich 26/4/40.
Stratford 30/4/47.
Colchester 10/5/47.
Stratford 6/12/59.

RENUMBERED:
7567 27/11/25.
5465 17/11/46.
65465 25/8/49.

CONDEMNED: 16/9/62.

7568

Stratford.

To traffic 4/1912.

REPAIRS:
Str. 15/8—7/11/19.**G.**
Str. 22/3—23/6/22.**G.**
Str. 9/5—6/9/24.**G.**
Str. 26/11/26—3/2/26.**G.**
Str. 20/3—24/5/29.**G.**
Coal guard on tender.
Str. 28/6—22/7/29.**H.**
Str. 11/9—2/11/31.**G.**
Str. 15/3—27/4/34.**G.**
Str. 9/5—10/6/36.**G.**
Str. 19/8—26/9/38.**G.**
Str. 25/1—20/2/41.**G.**
Trip cock gear fitted.
Str. 27/12/41—17/1/42.**L.**
Str. 2—16/9/42.**G.**
Str. 27/2—25/3/44.**G.**
Str. 19/5—21/6/46.**G.**
Str. 31/1—15/4/47.**L.**

Trip cock gear refitted.
Str. 7/9—5/10/48.**G.**
Str. 13—31/3/50.**C/H.**
Str. 16/3—14/4/51.**H/I.**
Str. 1—26/3/54.**G.**
Str. 20/2—14/3/57.**C/L.**

BOILERS:
568.
566 7/11/19.
2512 23/6/22.
2536 24/5/29.
2716 2/11/31.
2522 27/4/34.
2744 10/6/36.
2782 26/9/38.
3301 20/2/41.
3331 16/9/42.
2550 25/3/44.
2790 21/6/46.
3374 5/10/48.
2788 31/3/50.
2788 reno.23517 14/4/51.
23528 26/3/54.

SHEDS:
Ipswich.
Colchester by 1/1/35.
Stratford 20/7/41.
Colchester 19/1/46.
Stratford 10/5/47.
Colchester 21/6/53.

RENUMBERED:
7568 6/9/24.
5466 24/11/46.
65466 2/10/48.

CONDEMNED: 28/7/58.
Cut up at Stratford.

7569

Stratford.

To traffic 4/1912.

REPAIRS:
Str. 8/1—22/2/16.**G.**
Str. 10/3—20/5/20.**G.**
Str. 9/11/22—24/3/23.**G.**
Str. 7/2—6/5/25.**G.**
Str. 23/4—2/7/27.**G.**
Str. 4/1—8/2/30.**G.**
Coal guard on tender.
Str. 18/3—8/4/31.**G.**
Str. 10/8—7/9/32.**G.**
Str. 27/9—17/10/34.**G.**
Str. 3/1—3/2/37.**G.**
Str. 29/1—12/3/40.**G.**
Str. 14/8—1/10/43.**G.**
Str. 23/9—6/10/45.**G.**
Str. 27/2—5/4/48.**G.**
Str. 11/6—28/7/51.**G.**

7569 cont./
Str. 17/4—13/5/55.**G.**

BOILERS:
569.
2515 22/2/16.
552 20/5/20.
554 24/3/23.
641 6/5/25.
2517 2/7/27.
563 8/2/30.
2545 7/9/32.
2509 17/10/34.
2542 3/2/37.
2768 12/3/40.
2571 1/10/43.
3342 6/10/45.
3396 5/4/48.
23522 28/7/51.
23588 13/5/55.

SHEDS:
Ipswich.
March 20/6/28.
Ipswich 11/10/28.
Stratford 3/2/57.

RENUMBERED:
7569 6/5/25.
5467 17/11/46.
65467 3/4/48.

CONDEMNED: 3/2/59.
Cut up at Stratford.

7570

Stratford.

To traffic 5/1912.

REPAIRS:
YEC. 8/12/19—8/12/20.**G.**
Cam. 2/1—31/3/22.**H.**
Str. 25/2—24/5/24.**G.**
Str. 15/10—7/12/26.**G.**
Str. 15/12/28—14/2/29.**G.**
Coal guard on tender.
Str. 10/11—30/12/31.**G.**
Str. 7/4—26/5/34.**G.**
Str. 13/12/36—14/1/37.**G.**
Str. 30/6—22/7/38.**H.**
Str. 24/12/39—6/2/40.**G.**
Str. 22/12/42—4/2/43.**G.**
Str. 25/2—16/3/45.**G.**
Str. 16/5—20/6/47.**G.**
Str. 1—25/3/49.**C/H.**
Str. 30/8—16/9/50.**G.**
Str. 18/12/52—10/1/53.**G.**
Str. 6/3—7/4/56.**G.**

BOILERS:
570.
544 7/12/26.

2536 30/12/31.
2542 26/5/34.
3309 14/1/37.
3302 22/7/38.
2519 6/2/40.
2744 4/2/43.
3366 16/3/45.
2578 20/6/47.
2768 25/3/49.
23500 16/9/50.
23572 10/1/53.
23534 7/4/56.

SHEDS:
Cambridge.
March 17/6/34.
Cambridge 16/10/34.
Stratford 2/5/47.
Colchester 25/6/50.

RENUMBERED:
7570 24/5/24.
5468 17/11/46.
65468 25/3/49.

CONDEMNED: 30/9/59.
Cut up at Stratford.

7571

Stratford.

To traffic 5/1912.

REPAIRS:
Str. 15/2—25/6/18.**G.**
Str. 2/11/23—14/2/24.**G.**
Str. 31/7—3/12/26.**G.**
Str. 29/1—16/4/29.**G.**
Coal guard on tender.
Str. 21/10—15/12/31.**G.**
Str. 2—26/5/33.**H.**
Str. 23/4—28/6/34.**G.**
Str. 27/8—15/9/36.**G.**
Str. 9/1—10/2/39.**G.**
Str. 16/7—26/8/39.**H.**
Str. 24/2—22/3/41.**G.**
Str. 6/2—9/3/43.**G.**
Str. 11/2—3/3/45.**G.**
Str. 12/12/47—25/1/48.**G.**
Str. 12/11—2/12/50.**G.**
Str. 16/1—21/2/53.**G.**
Str. 5/5—7/6/57.**G.**

BOILERS:
571.
910 25/6/18.
569 14/2/24.
2673 16/4/29.
569 15/12/31.
2766 28/6/34.
3315 15/9/36.
2554 10/2/39.
2783 22/3/41.

2573 9/3/43.
3335 3/3/45.
2580 25/1/48.
23504 2/12/50.
23574 21/2/53.
23506 7/6/57.

SHEDS:
Cambridge.
Stratford 5/6/38.
Norwich 6/9/40.
Lowestoft 16/4/44.
Norwich 30/7/44.
Lowestoft 19/11/44.
Yarmouth 7/9/45.
Norwich 19/3/47.
Yarmouth 20/8/47.
Yarmouth Beach 19/10/47.
Norwich 4/2/48.
Lowestoft 30/6/57.
Norwich 8/9/57.
Cambridge 10/9/61.
March 17/6/62.

RENUMBERED:
7571 14/2/24.
5469 24/11/46.
ᴇ5469 25/1/48.
65469 2/12/50.

CONDEMNED: 1/8/62.

7542

Stratford.

To traffic 6/1913.

REPAIRS:
Str. 12/1—31/3/20.**G.**
Nor. 1/2—28/3/24.**H.**
Str. 7/4—3/8/26.**G.**
Str. 15/1—26/3/29.**G.**
Coal guard on tender.
Str. 10/8—23/9/31.**G.**
Str. 29/8—27/9/33.**G.**
Str. 15/3—30/4/37.**G.**
Str. 9/10—27/11/39.**G.**
Str. 20/2—20/3/43.**G.**
Str. 24/6—2/8/45.**G.**
Str. 18/11—23/12/47.**G.**
Str. 19/7—12/8/50.**G.**
Str. 21/6—27/7/51.**C/L.**
Str. 23/7—23/8/52.**C/H.**
Str. 29/1—28/2/53.**G.**
Str. 12/6—3/8/56.**G.**

BOILERS:
542.
545 31/3/20.
2547 3/8/26.
2716 26/3/29.
2743 23/9/31.
2577 27/9/33.

2689 30/4/37.
3321 27/11/39.
3303 20/3/43.
2580 2/8/45.
3308 23/12/47.
3309 12/8/50.
3309 reno.23525 27/7/51.
23500 28/2/53.
23568 3/8/56.

SHEDS:
Yarmouth.
Norwich 12/1/29.
March 23/6/30.
Norwich 29/8/30.
Ipswich 26/4/34.
Colchester 15/11/34.
Norwich 16/1/35.
Yarmouth 31/5/36.
Norwich 31/3/37.
Yarmouth 30/7/39.
Norwich 3/9/39.
Lowestoft 1/12/40.
Norwich 5/4/42.
Yarmouth 18/7/43.
Norwich 10/10/43.
Yarmouth 30/6/46.
Norwich 24/11/46.
Ipswich 6/6/48.
Norwich 21/7/48.
Melton Constable 3/10/48.
Norwich 17/10/48.
Ipswich 27/3/49.
Colchester 12/11/50.

RENUMBERED:
7542 28/3/24 ?
5470 1/12/46.
65470 12/8/50.

CONDEMNED: 7/12/59.
Cut up at Stratford.

7543

Stratford.

To traffic 6/1913.

REPAIRS:
Str. 18/11/20—18/2/21.**G.**
Nor. 3/9—3/11/23.**H.**
Nor. 6—15/6/24.**L.**
Str. 3/6—17/10/25.**G.**
Str. 19/1—28/4/28.**G.**
Coal guard on tender.
Str. 28/5—18/7/30.**G.**
Str. 8/5—2/6/33.**G.**
Str. 22/10—14/11/35.**G.**
Str. 2/6—7/7/37.**G.**
Str. 18/9—4/11/39.**G.**
Str. 20/1—19/3/43.**G.**
Str. 18/3—12/4/45.**G.**
Str. 31/8—8/10/47.**G.**

In 1958 the last three general repairs were made to: 65457 (15th March), 65445 (22nd March), and 65460 (14th April). Cambridge, 2nd May 1959.

(*below*) No.65476 did visit Stratford works 22nd to 30th October 1958, for repairs to its tender only which then got the BR crest. Note the electrification warning flash put on the engine. Tottenham, 21st August 1962.

This engine met with earlier trouble with its tender. When ex works 2nd February 1952, its own tender No.7569 was not ready and for a few days it ran with 7642, which was a spare and still had the lettering which had been discarded in 1949. T7642 was repaired and then used by E4 class No.62781 from 29th March 1952 to 2nd January 1956. Stratford works, 3rd February 1952.

In the 1950's the pipe along the angle iron, feeding the carriage heating connection at the front end, was found to need insulation. The first attempts at wrapping it (*see* page 64, centre) were insufficient so a sheet metal tube was put on.

(*above*) No.65388 two weeks after its withdrawal on 22nd May 1959. Note that though only a steam brake was fitted, a screw coupling, shorter chimney and high tender cab are in evidence. The paint condition resulted from its last visit to works being 12th June 1953. Stratford shed.

No.65477, in May 1959, was one of at least eight J15's fitted with a hand wheel controlled stop valve on the front plate of the cab. It was used for clearing ice and snow from points and could be used as an auxiliary water pump. Other J15's similarly fitted were: 7941, 65391, 5424, 65438, 5454, 65475 and 65476. Cambridge, 2nd May 1959.

7543 cont./
Str. 6—19/11/49.**G.**
Str. 1—24/2/51.**C/L.**
Str. 8/6—4/7/52.**G.**
Str. 11/3—3/5/56.**G.**

BOILERS:
543.
2552 18/2/21.
2501 28/4/28.
545 18/7/30.
2567 2/6/33.
2781 14/11/35.
2577 7/7/37.
2544 4/11/39.
3344 19/3/43.
3368 8/10/47.
3358 19/11/49.
3358 reno.23510 24/2/51.
23556 4/7/52.
23538 3/5/56.

SHEDS:
Norwich.
Lowestoft 17/12/35.
Norwich 25/2/36.
Lowestoft 23/5/37.
Norwich 9/6/37.
Lowestoft 20/9/41.
Ipswich 19/11/44.
Norwich 14/6/45.
Lowestoft 20/10/45.
Norwich 20/2/47.
Lowestoft 12/10/49.
Norwich 4/12/49.

RENUMBERED:
7543 17/10/25.
5471 1/9/46.
65471 19/11/49.

CONDEMNED: 17/6/60.
Cut up at Stratford.

7544

Stratford.

To traffic 6/1913.

REPAIRS:
Str. 21/12/20—2/3/21.**G.**
Nor. 31/10—20/12/22.**H.**
Str. 11/10/24—3/1/25.**G.**
Str. 3/1—16/4/27.**G.**
Coal guard on tender.
Str. 19/12/29—25/1/30.**G.**
Str. 22/5—24/6/32.**G.**
Str. 7/8—21/9/34.**G.**
Str. 16/8—9/9/35.**H.**
Str. 18/6—28/7/37.**G.**
Str. 6/8—19/9/39.**G.**
Str. 30/4—3/6/42.**G.**
Str. 8/10—3/11/44.**G.**

Str. 14/9—15/11/47.**G.**
Str. 19/10—20/11/48.**L.**
Str. 5—20/5/50.**G.**
Str. 7/6—2/7/53.**G.**
Str. 19/5—24/6/57.**G.**

BOILERS:
544.
2553 2/3/21.
2517 3/1/25.
570 16/4/27.
2511 25/1/30.
2509 24/6/32.
3321 21/9/34.
3319 28/7/37.
2772 19/9/39.
3310 3/6/42.
3361 3/11/44.
2761 20/5/50.
23579 2/7/53.
23586 24/6/57.

SHEDS:
Norwich.
March 20/6/28.
Norwich 7/8/28.
Yarmouth 12/1/29.
Norwich 3/8/30.
Yarmouth 18/10/31.
Norwich 10/7/32.
Yarmouth 7/11/33.
Norwich 17/3/34.
Melton Constable 21/2/43.
Norwich 29/8/45.
Melton Constable 17/9/45.
Norwich 13/9/46.
Melton Constable 29/9/46.
Norwich 23/3/47.
Yarmouth Beach 17/12/47.
Norwich 5/3/48.
Cambridge 20/5/51.
Norwich 10/6/51.
Ipswich 1/1/56.
Norwich 25/3/56.
Yarmouth 7/7/57.
Norwich 15/9/57.
Colchester 17/8/58.
Stratford 29/11/59.

RENUMBERED:
7544 3/1/25.
5472 21/12/46.
65472 20/11/48.

CONDEMNED: 7/12/59.
Cut up at Stratford.

7545

Stratford.

To traffic 6/1913.

REPAIRS:
Str. 31/10/19—13/3/20.**G.**
Str. 11/2—1/6/21.**G.**
Ips. 22/1—21/3/23.**H.**
Str. 2/7—7/10/25.**G.**
Str. 7/3—19/5/28.**G.**
Coal guard on tender.
Str. 1/10—7/11/30.**G.**
Str. 12/11—15/12/33.**G.**
Str. 8/4—4/5/36.**G.**
Str. 11—22/12/37.**G.**
Str. 16/1—21/2/40.**G.**
Str. 20/6—24/8/43.**G.**
Str. 26/8—15/9/45.**G.**
Str. 27/5—30/6/48.**G.**
Str. 4/2—3/3/51.**G.**
Str. 1/7—1/8/53.**G.**
Str. 19—22/10/53.**N/C.**
Str. 10/12/56—5/1/57.**G.**

BOILERS:
545.
553 13/3/20.
543 1/6/21.
554 7/10/25.
645 7/11/30.
3312 15/12/33.
2724 4/5/36.
3304 22/12/37.
3326 21/2/40.
2786 24/8/43.
2788 15/9/45.
3364 30/6/48.
23512 3/3/51.
23580 1/8/53.
23567 5/1/57.

SHEDS:
Ipswich.
Yarmouth Beach 26/7/42.
Norwich 7/3/43.
Yarmouth 28/10/45.
Norwich 5/3/46.
Stratford 24/4/47.
Colchester 10/5/47.
Stratford 6/12/59.

RENUMBERED:
7545 7/10/25.
5473 12/1/47.
65473 26/6/48.

CONDEMNED: 17/3/60.
Cut up at Stratford.

7546

Stratford.

To traffic 7/1913.

REPAIRS:
Str. 28/5—17/8/20.**G.**
Str. 27/7—4/11/22.**G.**

Str. 17/1—14/3/25.**G.**
Str. 4/3—27/5/27.**G.**
Str. 29/10—29/12/28.**G.**
Coal guard on tender.
Str. 6/6—23/7/31.**G.**
Str. 18/2—16/3/34.**G.**
Str. 29/2—2/4/36.**G.**
Str. 15/6—16/7/38.**G.**
Str. 29/4—4/6/41.**G.**
Str. 7/5—10/6/44.**G.**
Str. 17—26/7/45.**L.**
Str. 4/8—22/9/46.**G.**
Str. 7/4—14/5/49.**G.**
Str. 9/12/51—4/1/52.**G.**
Str. 15/2—24/3/55.**G.**

BOILERS:
546.
554 17/8/20.
548 4/11/22.
550 29/12/28.
2542 23/7/31.
2533 16/3/34.
3302 2/4/36.
2767 16/7/38.
3305 4/6/41.
3351 10/6/44.
3379 22/9/46.
3353 14/5/49.
23539 4/1/52.
23544 24/3/55.

SHEDS:
Ipswich.
Stratford 25/1/29.
Southend 14/12/29.
Stratford 28/12/29.
Southend 4/1/30.
Stratford 15/3/30.
Southend 22/3/30.
Stratford 29/3/30.
Southend 5/4/30.
Stratford 26/4/30.
Southend 3/5/30.
Stratford 14/6/30.
Southend 21/6/30.
Stratford 28/6/30.
Southend 2/8/30.
Stratford 9/8/30.
Southend 15/11/30.
Stratford *by* 1/1/35.
Cambridge 25/8/38.
Bury St Edmunds 24/6/42.
Cambridge 15/7/42.
March 29/5/55.

RENUMBERED:
7546 14/3/25.
5474 8/12/46.
65474 14/5/49.

CONDEMNED: 8/2/60.
Cut up at Stratford.

7547

Stratford.

To traffic 8/1913.

REPAIRS:
Pbo. 31/1—29/3/23.**H.**
Str. 18/5—20/8/25.**G.**
Str. 26/1—12/4/28.**G.**
Coal guard on tender.
Str. 23/10—14/11/30.**G.**
Str. 8—29/9/32.**G.**
Str. 17/7—13/9/34.**G.**
Str. 16/6—9/8/37.**G.**
Str. 3/11—4/12/39.**G.**
Trip cock gear fitted.
Str. 31/10—7/12/42.**G.**
Str. 19—31/8/45.**G.**
Str. 30/5—28/6/46.**L.**
Str. 24—27/3/47.**N/C.**
Trip cock gear re-fitted.
Str. 15/12/47—11/2/48.**G.**
Str. 4—23/9/50.**G.**
Str. 14/6—3/7/53.**G.**
Str. 23/7—22/9/56.**G.**

BOILERS:
547.
567 12/4/28.
2550 14/11/30.
2793 29/9/32.
3319 13/9/34.
2566 9/8/37.
2558 4/12/39.
3336 7/12/42.
3346 31/8/45.
3343 11/2/48.
23501 23/9/50.
23519 3/7/53.
23564 22/9/56.

SHEDS:
Peterborough East.
Stratford 31/1/31.
Colchester 19/1/46.
Stratford 10/5/47.
Cambridge 3/7/49.
Colchester 1/9/49.
Cambridge 4/11/49.

RENUMBERED:
7547 20/8/25.
5475 3/1/47.
E5475 11/2/48.
65475 23/9/50.

CONDEMNED: 1/9/59.
Cut up at Stratford.

7548

Stratford.

To traffic 8/1913.

REPAIRS:
Str. 28/2—18/6/21.**G.**
Cam. 21/9—26/10/23.**H.**
Str. 20/2—23/5/25.**G.**
Str. 27/8—2/12/27.**G.**
Coal guard on tender.
Str. 19/2—29/3/30.**G.**
Str. 3—28/5/32.**G.**
Str. 11/2—15/3/35.**G.**
Str. 23/4/35—2/5/35.**L.**
Str. 26/10—16/11/37.**G.**
Str. 7/6—4/7/40.**G.**
Trip cock gear fitted.
Str. 17/1—27/2/43.**G.**
Str. 5—24/8/45.**G.**
Str. 24—27/3/47.**N/C.**
Trip cock gear re-fitted.
Str. 5—23/12/47.**H.**
Str. 18/10—9/12/48.**G.**
Str. 26/6—22/7/50.**C/H.**
Str. 3—19/8/50.**C/L.**
Str. 9/5/51.**C/L.**
Str. 14/1—2/2/52.**G.**
Str. 8/9—20/10/56.**G.**
Str. 22—30/10/58.*Tender only.*

BOILERS:
548.
550 18/6/21.
2545 23/5/25.
2543 2/12/27.
2509 29/3/30.
2512 28/5/32.
3304 15/3/35.
2789 16/11/37.
3302 4/7/40.
3342 27/2/43.
3343 24/8/45.
3373 23/12/47.
3363 22/7/50.
23542 2/2/52.
23519 20/10/56.

SHEDS:
Cambridge .
King's Lynn 5/11/29.
Cambridge 10/11/29.
Stratford 10/7/40.
Parkeston 19/1/46.
Stratford 10/5/47.
Colchester 11/2/51.
Stratford 17/6/51.

RENUMBERED:
7548 23/5/25.
5476 28/10/46.
65476 4/12/48.

CONDEMNED: 5/9/62.

Sold for scrap to J.Cashmore, Great Bridge, 11/62.

7549

Stratford.

To traffic 8/1913.

REPAIRS:
Str. 26/4—13/8/20.**G.**
Str. 3/12/23—2/4/24.**G.**
Str. 23/7—10/12/26.**G.**
Coal guard on tender.
Str. 11/4—24/7/28.**G.**
Str. 30/4—18/6/30.**G.**
Str. 17/5—13/6/32.**G.**
Str. 13/9—12/10/34.**G.**
Str. 15/12/36—28/1/37.**G.**
Str. 10/9—23/10/39.**G.**
Str. 16/6—13/7/42.**H/I.**
Str. 19/5—30/6/44.**G.**
Str. 12/2—8/3/46.**G.**
Str. 8/4—29/5/48.**G.**
Str. 25/3—19/4/51.**G.**
Str. 30/11/53—1/1/54.**C/H.**
Str. 4/3—18/4/57.**G.**

BOILERS:
549.
2515 13/8/20.
644 2/4/24.
562 10/12/26.
2569 24/7/28.
2561 18/6/30.
2780 13/6/32.
2558 28/1/37.
3328 23/10/39.
3305 30/6/44.
2570 8/3/46.
3398 29/5/48.
23518 19/4/51.
23506 1/1/54.
23555 18/4/57.

SHEDS:
Cambridge .
King's Lynn 19/8/45.
Cambridge 11/2/46.

RENUMBERED:
7549 2/4/24.
5477 1/12/46.
65477 29/5/48.

CONDEMNED: 8/2/60.
Cut up at Stratford.

7550

Stratford.

To traffic 9/1913.

REPAIRS:
Str. 10/9—19/11/20.**G.**
Str. 16/5—21/7/23.**G.**
Str. 1/7—24/9/25.**G.**
Str. 16/6—5/9/28.**G.**
Coal guard on tender.
Str. 12/3—9/5/31.**G.**
Str. 18/7—18/8/33.**G.**
Str. 19/2—19/3/36.**G.**
Str. 15/11—19/12/38.**G.**
Str. 12/10—14/11/42.**G.**
Str. 21/1—9/2/45.**G.**
Str. 24/3—22/4/47.**G.**
Str. 17/8—10/9/49.**G.**
Str. 26/4—23/5/53.**G.**
Str. 27/6—10/8/57.**G.**

BOILERS:
550.
2500 19/11/20.
2506 5/9/28.
2571 9/5/31.
3305 18/8/33.
2554 19/3/36.
2580 19/12/38.
3335 14/11/42.
3310 9/2/45.
2569 22/4/47.
3320 10/9/49.
23571 23/5/53.
23575 10/8/57.

SHEDS:
Stratford.
Norwich 3/10/24.
Stratford 6/12/24.
Cambridge 24/6/26.
Stratford 23/10/26.
Norwich 4/1/29.
March 23/6/30.
Norwich 30/8/30.
Lowestoft 6/2/49.
Norwich 9/3/49.
Lowestoft 30/7/50.
Ipswich 1/3/59.
Cambridge 13/3/60.

RENUMBERED:
7550 24/9/25.
5478 1/12/46.
65478 10/9/49.

CONDEMNED: 26/10/61.
To Doncaster for c/u 26/10/61.

7551

Stratford.

To traffic 9/1913.

REPAIRS:
Str. 12/10/17—29/1/18.**G.**
Str. 12/11/20—19/1/21.**G.**

7551 cont./
Str. 9/5—17/8/23.**G.**
Str. 24/12/25—25/3/26.**G.**
Str. 30/11/28—17/1/29.**G.**
Coal guard on tender.
Str. 19/4—22/5/31.**G.**
Str. 20/5—22/6/33.**G.**
Str. 2—31/1/35.**G.**
Str. 12/7—13/8/37.**G.**
Str. 31/8—18/10/39.**G.**
Str. 5/12/42—9/1/43.**G.**
Str. 31/12/44—20/1/45.**G.**
Str. 24/6—10/9/46.**G.**
Str. 7—27/12/48.**G.**
Str. 5—29/12/51.**G.**
Str. 4—28/10/55.**G.**

BOILERS:
 551.
 556 29/1/18.
 2547 19/1/21.
 565 17/8/23.
 564 25/3/26.
 2523 17/1/29.
 2562 22/5/31.
 3304 22/6/33.
 2545 31/1/35.
 3321 13/8/37.
 3319 18/10/39.
 2580 9/1/43.
 3339 20/1/45.
 2795 10/9/46.
 3336 27/12/48.
 23538 29/12/51.
 23557 28/10/55.

SHEDS:
Stratford.
Norwich 3/10/24.
Stratford 6/12/24.
Cambridge 23/6/26.
Stratford 15/12/26.
Cambridge 11/6/27.
Stratford 28/9/27.
March 19/6/28.
Stratford 15/10/28.
Norwich 29/1/29.
Yarmouth 9/3/35.
Norwich 22/4/35.
Lowestoft 6/5/35.
Norwich 20/5/35.
Ipswich 29/11/45.
Norwich 7/4/46.
Lowestoft 3/10/48.
Norwich 9/1/49.
Colchester 12/11/50.
Hitchin 21/6/53.

RENUMBERED:
 7551 25/3/26.
 5479 1/12/46.
 65479 24/12/48.

CONDEMNED: 15/8/60.
To Doncaster for c/u 15/8/60.

The last boiler with Ross 'pop' safety valves on a Ramsbottom base, was taken off No.65366 when withdrawn in June 1952. It had started work in April 1930 on No.7843. To that batch washout plugs were fitted. Note that when a snowplough was fitted, the front buffers were taken off (*see also* page 45, centre). Cambridge, 31st March 1952.

Later boilers, with safety valves mounted on the firebox, had inspection holes - two on each side - which served also for washout purposes. Stratford, 18th March 1950.

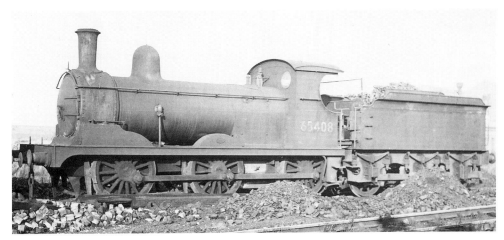

Fitting of tablet exchange apparatus was rare on J15 but No.65408 had it when it was No.7915. That engine was only at an M&GN shed, Yarmouth Beach, from 30th April 4th June 1944, going there from, and then back to Norwich. Stratford, December 1951.

No.65435, ex works 22nd August 1952, still had two lamp irons at the right hand front end, but was also unusual in not having a number plate on smokebox. Note the 1924 load class 3 plate is still on the buffer beam with the 1947-introduced R.A.1 painted on the cab side. Stratford, August 1952.

No.7690 was sold on the 7th June 1938 to Bairds & Scottish Steel Ltd., and remained in service with that company until 1960 when it was scrapped. From 3rd October to 27th December 1945 it was in Cowlairs works for a general repair and a change of boiler. Note the polished brass dome cover and parallel stovepipe chimney, also the displacement lubricators on the smokebox front, none of which were Great Eastern features.

The last engines in the class were Nos.65361, 65462, 65464, and 65465, all withdrawn on 16th September 1962. No.65462, originally GER No.564 of March 1912, was purchased by the M&GN Joint Railway preservation society for restoration to running order at Sheringham.